Discovering Annuals

Graham Rice

Discovering Annuals

Timber Press
Portland, Oregon

Graham Rice: Discovering Annuals
Copyright © Frances Lincoln Limited 1999
Text copyright © Graham Rice 1999

Published in North America in 1999 by
Timber Press, Inc.
The Haseltine Building
133 S.W. Second Avenue, Suite 450
Portland, Oregon 97204, U.S.A.

A catalogue record for this book is available from the Library of Congress.

ISBN 0-88192-465-2

Set in Hiroshige
Printed in Hong Kong by Kwong Fat

2 4 6 8 9 7 5 3 1

HALF TITLE PAGE *Three pink annuals from a color-themed seed mixture:* Iberis
'Red Flash', Collomia grandiflora 'Neon' *and* Silene 'Rose Angel'

TITLE PAGE *'Gallery Yellow' perennial lupines surge through the yellow foliage
and white daisies of* Tanacetum parthenium *'Aureum, while the purple
foliage of* Plantago major *'Rubrifolia' creates contrast.*

FAR RIGHT *The wild form of the pot marigold,* Calendula officinalis, *with
its unusually reddish eye, peeps through* Alchemilla mollis *while a
small-flowered blue viola fills in behind.*

Contents

What are annuals?

It's an unusual book, you have to admit, which feels the need to devote a specific page to ensuring that its readers understand what the book they've just opened is actually about. But "annual" is one of those words which seems to create a haze of uncertainty among gardeners so it seems wise to set things straight – although, as you will soon see, "straight" is hardly the word for it.

Ask the botanists and they will probably tell you that an annual is a plant the seed of which germinates, and that develops flowers, produces its own seed, and then dies all in one year; they may say it all takes place over a "course of seasons".

So most annuals germinate in the spring, flower in late spring and summer, and die in the late summer or autumn; alyssum, clarkia, and zinnia are familiar examples. A few, however, can also behave as winter annuals, germinating in the late summer and autumn then remaining partially dormant over the winter before starting into growth again in spring and completing their cycle in summer. Annual chrysanthemum from the Mediterranean fall into this group.

Now the situation becomes rather less clear. For many of the plants which we grow in gardens as annuals, plants like petunias and salvias, are not truly annuals at all. Usually these are shrubs or perennials from warm climates which, once they germinate in spring, develop so quickly that they flower well in their first summer. In many zones, they're not sufficiently tough to survive the autumn frosts so are quickly wiped out.

Both these groups – true annuals and those plants which can be grown as annuals – are included in this book, along with a third smaller group of short-lived plants, the biennials. Like annuals, biennials usually pass through their entire life cycle in one "course of seasons" but their growth is always spread across two years. So their seed germinates in summer, established plants overwinter, then flower in spring.

Now, at the risk of adding further confusion, it must be admitted that many of the plants we grow as biennials are, in their natural habitats, perennials or shrubs! However, when sown in summer, plants like wallflowers and double daisies have the capacity to flower so prolifically in their first spring, that we naturally take advantage.

Finally (yes, finally) a few biennials, like some foxgloves and sweet Williams, have been so transformed by plant breeders that when sown in late winter or early spring they flower in their first summer – as annuals! This only applies to certain specific varieties, and frankly, turning some of our relatively few spring-flowering bedding plants into summer flowers (of which we already have so many) hardly seems progress.

All these various groups are discussed in this book. All are raised from seed and, at the time of writing, all are available from the mail-order seed companies listed at the back of the book.

LEFT *The bold black Tuscan kale, 'Nero di Toscana', is surrounded by flowers which pick up its dark coloring. Yellow-throated* Nolana paradoxa *(an unusual petunia-like plant from Chile) creeps underneath,* Salvia farinacea *'Strata' peeps through the spaces and* Nemesia *'KLM' snuggles into* Senecio cineraria *'Silver Dust'.*

RIGHT *This happy conjunction of bluish flowers, all from a direct sowing in the open ground of a blue-themed mixture, features three different phacelias together with echiums, annual flax and bachelor buttons.*

LEFT *Some of the best color-themed plantings are the result of thoughtful planning. Here,* Nicotiana sylvestris *is set in the middle ground to open in front of white hydrangeas and among the Shasta daises (*Leucanthemum x superbum*) while white petunias fill the foreground under the silver leaves of* Convolvulus cneorom.

Catching the Wave

There's an old song by the Beach Boys called "Catch a Wave." The point of the song is that when you're out in the surf, waiting for a wave to come, you must choose the right wave and exactly the right moment to grab the best chance of riding the crest all the way in. "Seize the day." "Hit the ground running" . . . there are other metaphors for the same sort of thing. The point is this: annuals have been in a dead calm for years, but now their moment has come.

But let's stop here for a minute. "Annual" is a term which covers most temporary plants, whether planted for a summer in Maine or a winter in Florida. Some are raised from seed, either at home or by a nursery, and some are propagated vegetatively, from cuttings. This book features the vast range of seed-raised annuals, combining as they do the richest source of variety with availability. A packet of seed is easy to send in the mail, to and from anywhere in the world, but cuttings and plants suffer in the mail – even supposing that your state will allow them in at all. It's a mistake to depend on your local nursery to stock the same varieties even from month to month, never mind from year to year; seed companies are more dependable. This book is written with seed in mind, although you will find some of these varieties as plants in the garden center or occasionally in mail-order catalogs.

Seed-raised annuals spent a long period out of fashion. Tainted by association with gaudy bedding schemes in public parks, all were dismissed and many despised. But a change of spirit is taking place, a change which mirrors our times, a change ignited by enthusiasm for carefully planned color schemes in the garden and by enthusiasm for container plants like Supertunias. And that's the key to it all: change.

We've reached a time when change –

rapid and dramatic – is a feature of our lives like never before. We've responded in two ways. We look to preserve elements of stability in our lives and, at the same time, we learn not to battle against change, but to thrive on it.

It's possible to see the results of these reactions, these two complementary elements of our adaptability, in our gardens. Gardeners have become more interested in permanence. For example, there's a special fascination with large and long-lived trees. We are planting more trees and we plant fast-growing trees which quickly give an illusion of longevity. Even our enthusiasm for topiary and low box hedges is rooted in some inclination to replicate the old and long-established.

Gardeners are also making more connections with the past – investigating the origins of plants, reintroducing lost plants and in particular looking back to heritage gardens and even to England for old varieties, searching out old types for re-introduction, rediscovering native annual species, and wherever possible rescuing lost plants. Indeed, the enormous fascination for heirloom and native varieties, in particular of annuals and vegetables, shows the power of this feeling for the past. The revival and reintroduction of heirloom annuals has been a significant factor in encouraging enthusiastic gardeners to look beyond ghastly African marigolds to annuals with a more natural poise, annuals more akin to the perennials which have so gripped the attention of gardeners in recent decades.

And in looking beyond the familiar, gardeners have discovered a fascinating

LEFT *White alyssum,* Lobularia maritima, *makes a creeping backdrop for the floppy stems of the native American meadow foam,* Limnanthes douglasii.

LEFT *Flowers in the marigold colors make a bright yet satisfying association. In the front, 'Seven Star Red' triploid marigolds, which flower incessantly and age harmoniously, are backed by an unusual bronze-leaved foliage plant, a relative of the gunnera no less,* Haloragis erecta *'Wellington Bronze'. To its left* Bulbine annua, *from South Africa, makes vertical marks and to its right the large daisies of* Rudbeckia *'Toto' are overhung by the grayish foliage and pale flowers of annual chrysanthemum 'Primrose Gem'. At the back* Calendula *'Indian Prince', with its chestnut-backed petals, picks up a similar shade in the 'Mahogany Midget' coreopsis.*

range of less common species and varieties. Not all of these have found space in this book – it could have been twice the size – but they will be covered on the *Discovering Annuals* website (see page 186).

While looking for stability, permanence, and connections with the past, we're also responding to change by reveling in it. And of the full range of garden plants, annuals raised from seed best represent this change – for annuals demand change.

True annuals, and other plants grown as annuals, last only one growing season. Once planted, trees, shrubs, perennials, and most vine reappear in the same place every year, changing only by growing steadily larger, while annuals die at the end of the season. So it takes a great effort of will to make one year's planting at all similar to that of the previous year. This chance to make each year's planting of annuals different makes growing annuals so exciting.

Of course, there's no insistent imperative for each year's annual borders to be entirely different; it's just that when the plants must be raised afresh from seed, there's an annual opportunity to grow something different. The most successful elements of one year's planting can be repeated or adapted, those which worked less well can be abandoned, and a new scheme can integrate the best of both.

But if there was nothing more to annuals than the fact that they died every autumn, no one would grow them. Of course there's more, and first among many valuable qualities is color.

Using color

It's color – too much of it used with too little grace and a stunning lack of artistry – which has discouraged so many gardeners from growing annuals over the years. None of us enjoy the wrong varieties grown in the wrong place in the wrong way. But the right varieties grown in the *right* way . . .

The truth is that, especially among the mainstream annuals, there's a vast variety of colors and shades. The fact that one catalog lists well over a hundred different varieties of pansy is not a cause for complaint but for celebration, since however close in color and habit some of them may be, they are all actually different. And whatever color scheme you have in mind, whatever your preferences and dislikes, it's possible to choose exactly the shade you require. Far from lacking subtlety as is normally supposed, annuals are chock-full of it.

Consider marigolds. Although many are far too ugly to be tolerated in any garden, or in this book, within a very narrow spectrum of color from mahogany to palest lemon there's such a wealth of flower form and flower size, plant size and habit, as well as the many tiny differences in color, that it's possible to pick precisely the shade you need in the height you need and in an attractive form. And if the plan doesn't work out *exactly* right, you can try a variation the following year. If you're planning a special display it's even possible to experiment with a number of similar varieties one year and to choose precisely the right one for the year after. You can't do that with rhododendrons.

The use of single colors rather than mixtures is absolutely crucial. Mixtures are unpredictable in their color and color balance, and however they turn out the colors usually clash. It's impossible to plan precision planting schemes if you introduce the inherent unpredictability of a mixture. Would you go into a store and buy six mixed socks, chosen at random by somebody else? Of course not. Likewise annuals.

Buying annuals in individual colors gives you the control of planting you expect with perennials and bulbs, and allows you to create personal schemes which reflect your own taste and preferences. The problem is that the availability of these colors changes from year to year so gardeners are kept locked into the cycle of change whether we like it or not!

Most African marigolds may be ugly but there are individual varieties of annuals which are as beautiful and as entrancing as any plants usually considered more choice. The very sight of 'Heavenly Blue' morning glory makes me shiver with delight; if I were to grow just one summer annual, this would be the one. The pure white of 'Sonnet White' snapdragon is unrivaled, the delicate flecking on the flowers of *Agrostemma* 'Ocean Spray' is delightful, the tender variation in shade between pale lavender-pink and white in *Petunia* 'Misty Lilac Wave', especially when grown as ground cover, is deliciously cool and relaxing.

It's true that many of these plants are not available in garden centers where the emphasis in the limited range offered is often on mixtures, but mail-order sources offer a much wider range of single colors. There are so many seed companies around the country, and indeed around the world, that there's always the chance of turning up exactly the color you need. The problem is that catalogs may list a variety one year, the next year they may not. The varieties mentioned in this book are all currently available either from American seed companies, Canadian seed companies, from the increasing number of British seed companies who mail seeds to the US., or available for ordering online

from websites. But such is the speed of change that it's possible a few will have been de-listed even in the time between writing and publication! (You'll find advice about ordering seeds from British seed companies on the *Discovering Annuals* website at http://DiscoveringAnnuals.com–see page 186.)

Annuals for foliage

Flower color need not be the only focus, for annuals have many other fine qualities, especially foliage. The bold, rounded leaves of nasturtiums are attractive in themselves; variegated forms like 'Alaska' and 'Jewel of Africa' add cream and white speckling. The variegated snapdragon 'Powys Pride' has foliage streaked in cream; silver foliage appears in senecios, tanacetums and even in eschscholzias; ornamental beetroots, many semperflorens begonias, the tuberous begonias 'Midnight Beauties' and 'Non Stop Ornament', and the taller *Hibiscus acetosella* 'Red Shield' all feature dark foliage in the bronze or purple range. The new *Solenostemon* (*Coleus*) 'Palisandra' is almost black.

Edible plants, not normally considered especially ornamental, are among the most valuable of all foliage annuals. Red cabbage like 'Scarlet O'Hara', whose leaves are often more of a bluish shade, and purple Brussels sprouts are very useful; the new purple curly kale 'Redbor' is invaluable; the many colored-stemmed chards like the startling 'Bright Lights' mixture and separate colors in scarlet and white are good even when they go to flower; red lettuce like 'Red Salad Bowl', 'New Red Fire', 'Merlot', and 'Red Sails' hold their shape well before bolting but make amusing dark spires as they stretch. Crisply curled parsley is an old favorite.

LEFT *Crisp seed heads of false saffron,* Carthamus tinctorius, *make a bold autumnal statement while contrastingly dainty heads of* Gypsophila elegans *and the final fling from blue batchelor's buutons fill the background.*

RIGHT *In the rough-and-tumble of this pink, purple, and white planting,* Salvia viridis *'Claryssa Pink', with its long-lasting pink bracts, will slowly overwhelm the 'Oriental Night' alyssum, white candytuft, the bushy South African* Sutera *'Krysna Hills' and probably the empty spaces as well.*

Some annuals also boast good seed heads. Nigellas, opium poppies, columbines, hollyhocks, teasels, honesty, nicandra, verbascum – these all bring an extra dimension both to the autumn garden and to dried arrangements for the house.

Annuals are also prolific bloomers. It's true that some sacrifice elegance for a punch between the eyes but most annuals do produce a great many flowers. This is a characteristic breeders have encouraged in their creations for centuries and in most cases this is combined with a long flowering season. Many annuals are in flower when you plant them in late spring and continue to bloom until they die naturally or the frost kills them in the autumn. In warmer zones, planting in the fall for flowering almost into the height of summer is more appropriate; the combination of heat and humidity may be what finally finishes them off. Even those sown direct in the open garden may well flower six or eight weeks after sowing and continue for months.

Elegance – or the lack of it

This book is nothing if not realistic. Annuals inspire strong negative feelings in many gardeners – hatred, disdain, snobbishness or disregard and, I have to say, plain ignorance – and I've tackled them head-on. Some annuals are ugly. My solution: don't grow them – grow those which are beautiful, stylish and elegant instead.

The very fact that some annuals are simply too crudely garish offends many people – and quite rightly too. And the fact that many are mostly seen in thoughtless mixtures does them no favors. My solution: don't grow them – choose the separate colors you enjoy.

There's no point trying to hide the fact that some annuals are almost impressively inelegant. The squat, dumpy habit (those words often appear elsewhere in this book) of some varieties – most of them relatively modern – disqualifies them from serious consideration although, to be fair, they may develop a taller and more open habit in the warmest zones. But if in doubt don't grow them – grow the many more elegant varieties instead.

There's little mystique about many of the more familiar annuals, which perhaps explains why for some gardeners they excite no interest. It also explains, perhaps, the disproportionate enthusiasm, mine included, for the history-rich Victorian varieties which are being reintroduced, along with those of the 1920s and 1930s, and which feature throughout this book.

Intimate (not bedding) schemes

The factor which turns people's stomachs at the very mention of annuals and bedding plants is the singularly unimaginative way in which they're so often used, especially in public spaces. Filling a roadside planting with orange African marigolds, as I've seen more than once, certainly ensures that they're noticed. But

capturing our brief attention by way of offending even the very broadest definition of taste and discrimination is clearly counterproductive. Surely it's better that drivers take their eyes off the traffic because the roadside displays are so attractive and intriguing, rather than because they're blindingly garish. So, how should annuals be grown and in particular how should they be grown in gardens?

Replicas of such schemes are unsuited to today's gardens. Large blocks of bold colors sit uneasily in small spaces where they visually overpower everything else in the garden, often by virtue of their scale. And classic combinations in which a bed of scarlet geraniums is edged with white alyssum and blue lobelia jars horribly with the more subtle mixed borders which are a feature of so many modern gardens. The sheer brilliance of blocks of color dominates so totally that the more delicate colorings of perennials and shrubs and climbers retreat into oblivion. So the answer is to banish anything resembling old-fashioned bedding schemes, to reduce the scale of the plantings from those great bed-fulls of scarlet, and to avoid choosing garish color combinations and planting them in large blocks.

Instead, plantings should be on a much more intimate scale. Varieties with a slightly taller, more open and elegant habit should have priority over the dwarfer types which concentrate more color into a small space at the expense of grace and distinction. Each variety should be planted in smaller numbers; in some cases one is enough, in many cases three is ideal. If more are planted, they should never be set in a concentrated block but interplanted with two or three other varieties which extend beyond the boundary of the main block and into neighboring groups.

Plantings should be organized and maintained in such a way that, as they mature, the plants grow into one another and mingle intimately, creating an ever-changing tapestry of color associations, intricate conjunctions of form in both flowers and foliage and a display which changes its emphasis as the season develops. There's more excitement in one square yard of intimate planting than in a whole garden full of old-fashioned bedding.

There's also far more opportunity for gardeners to express their own individuality in plantings of this style. Once you start using small groups of a large number of different varieties there's space to try far more ideas.

The success of this style of planting depends on choosing the right varieties. As I said earlier, avoid mixtures unless they're formula mixtures in predetermined colors which can be guaranteed to fit in with the planned scheme. And even in cases where the choice seems clear – a pansy in lemon yellow, for example – you need to select carefully from the range of flower sizes and habits of growth available.

Color themes

One of the most striking and satisfying ways of planning intimate plantings is by color. In my experiments with color-themed plants one of the most successful was in the marigold colors: mahogany, rust, orange, deep yellow, gold, and primrose. Plants which fit here include French, triploid, "tagetes", and pot marigolds, rudbeckias, bidens, camissonias, annual chrysanthemums, zinnias, snapdragons, eschscholzias, pansies, coreopsis, gazanias and more. Foliage color comes from dark-leaved dahlias, haloragis, nasturtiums, red lettuce and ornamental beetroot.

Rose-pink, silver, and white work well, red and white too; blue-flowered plants come in less variety so blue and white plantings need to be on a smaller scale. But almost any combination of colors will work, even red, white, and blue, if the plants are chosen carefully and allowed to grow into one another, rather than kept resolutely separate.

Bicolored flowers, of which there are so many among the annuals, are a great boon. An individual flower featuring two different colors can connect visually with neighbors which relate to each of the two shades, providing links and transitions in more mixed plantings.

A few seed companies offer color-themed mixtures. The best provide over 100 different varieties in each color that are packeted by three height ranges to give the gardener better control in the garden. These are full of happy surprises with rare species jostling with both familiar and unknown varieties of better-known species in a constantly refreshing sequence of color.

RIGHT *New Guinea impatiens from seed are still developing, but the Java Series marks a significant improvement on Spectra and Firelake. In cool summer areas, they're best grown in a container on a sheltered patio, as here. Their companions are* Heuchera *'Palace Purple' and the sinuous stems and gray foliage of* Helichrysum petiolare *in front. Only overwintered specimens of the licorice plant usually flower and, although routinely raised from cuttings, it can also be raised from seed. 'Black Prince' snapdragon has been cut back after its first flowering and is again in bud. In somewhat warmer areas and in rich soil New Guinea impatiens will also thrive in sunny beds and borders.*

OVERLEAF *What a spectacle! This interplanting of tall annuals makes a captivating display with the sparse but stiffly upright* Verbena bonariensis *surging through* Cosmos *'Imperial Pink' and 'Helen Campbell' and 'Purple Queen' cleomes. All can be started in pots then carefully set out in the border to ensure the right degree of intermingling before planting. The cleomes often germinate best in fluctuating temperatures so may need individual sowing treatment.*

ABOVE *Two vegetables provide the structure here: the purple Brussels sprout 'Falstaff' with its colored veins is fronted by the ruby chard 'Vulcan',* Chrysanthemum segetum *'Prado' expands from either side; 'Night and Day' snapgdragon sneaks through; while in front* Nicotiana *'Lime Green' is almost too vigorous for neighboring mask flower,* Alonsoa *'Amber Queen'.*

FAR RIGHT *Annual meadows can be undeniably colorful and here calendulas in their trademark bright yellows and oranges are interrupted by Shirley poppies in occasional reds and pinks, and bachelor's buttons and echiums in deep blue. Next year, when they all self-sow, the color balance could be entirely different.*

Mixed plantings

Choosing annuals carefully also allows them to meld much better with plants of other types. A fat block of 'Blaze of Fire' salvias would look ridiculous in a mixed border; a smaller block of *Salvia coccinea* 'Lady in Red' has the elegance of habit and the balance of color against habit to fit perfectly. Never exclude annuals from mixed plantings on the assumption that they won't fit aesthetically; choose the varieties that do. These may be tall like 'Lady in Red', 'Mother of Pearl' poppies, *Eryngium giganteum,* or sunflowers; they may be dwarf and spreading like *Bidens* 'Golden Eye', nasturtiums, some of the newer pansies, and 'Breakaway Red' geraniums.

There are, it has to be said, some especially valuable companions for flowering annuals and these I frequently (forgive any over-enthusiasm) recommend here. These are plants whose color and habit allow them to intermingle with their neighbors so that they dance together rather than simply plod. The various forms of licorice plant are especially useful, the arching trails insinuating themselves through their companions, their openness of habit allowing nearby plants to return the compliment. The silver foliage of the familiar species is invaluable as is the lime-yellow of 'Limelight'. The yellow-centered silver leaves of 'Variegatum', and its neater form 'Roundabout', are also useful; the neater silver form 'Goring Silver', sometimes listed simply as 'Dwarf Form', is usually the best choice for containers. *Plecostachys serpyllifolia*, often listed as a *Helichrysum petiolare*, develops especially long sinuous branches.

Another immensely useful plant, the dark-leaved ornamental beetroot 'MacGregor's Favorite', combines relatively compact yet loose growth in an invaluable color. The enormous range of colors and color combinations of vegetatively propagated coleus also creates contrasts, harmonies, and links with a wide range of other plants.

This way of growing annuals in intimate harmonies and contrasts is not the only way. Annuals fit well with Mediterranean plants. Indeed, with a gravel mulch among cistus, euphorbias, brooms and other Mediterranean shrubs they can be all too free with their seedlings. Choose wild species, or varieties close in

style to them and they fit perfectly. Enthusiastic deadheading and the rigorous removal of wayward seedlings which appear in the wrong places is crucial.

The use of annuals in wildflower gardens is common practice, if only as temporary color while perennial wildflowers become established. Given the space, the results can be impressive. But each year's display can be startlingly unpredictable and this approach also demands a continual and sophisticated regime of deadheading, thinning seedlings, and adding new varieties. Such wild gardens are an enjoyable way to grow annuals if you not only have the space and time to devote to them but also if there

are other areas of the garden which can provide a more dependably satisfying display.

However, the point of this book is to show that, in small gardens in particular, annuals need to be chosen carefully and planted with thoughtful precision to bring colors and forms together in combinations which allow the expression of the gardener's own character and taste. And, frankly, if you enjoy growing annuals in ways about which I do not enthuse in these pages – take no notice of me . . . plant your annuals in your own way. In so doing, we'll all continue to rediscover and reinvent the continuously changing pleasure of annuals.

Ageratum *Ageratum*

Blue is a rare and therefore precious color among annuals and we fall gratefully upon those few we have. So ageratums are invaluable – provided always that you choose carefully. But there are two problems.

Ageratum blue reproduces badly in photographs – the camera cannot lie but the film certainly can. Where there should be blue there is mauve, and where there should be mauve there is also mauve. So in books and catalogs, we find pictures that are either an unnaturally lurid blue thanks to computer manipulation . . . or mauve. It makes choosing difficult.

What's more, there are few varieties, other than those here, worth growing because again the plant breeder has ignored the gardener. What use are plants which reach little more than 6 in./15 cm. across and 4 in./10 cm. high in a whole season? Four varieties break this sad rule.

'Blue Horizon' is a valuable, cultured, slightly airy plant reaching about 2½ ft./ 75 cm., its flowers naturally tinted purple. With *Salvia farinacea* 'Victoria', 'Redbor' kale, and the sadly uncommon *Salpiglossis* 'Kew Blue', it makes a pretty grouping. Its white and "red" sisters are not yet listed in the U.S. but can be ordered from Europe. Whites can be disappointing; as the florets age to brown they detract from the pure

white of the fresher flowers, although in 'Highness' this is a less of a problem than with tiny edging sorts. In 'Red Sea' the buds are red, but the open flowers develop purplish tones. 'Blue Horizon', 'Highness' and 'Red Sea' are all triploid varieties, sterile hybrids which flower prolifically in their fruitless struggle to produce seed.

Coming down in scale as far as we'll go, 'Blue Mink' is an old favorite which sometimes varies a little in height but, at 9–12 in./23–30 cm. and with its slightly open habit, is the best blue for frontal plantings. Better still, yet at about the same height, is 'Southern Cross', also known as 'Bavaria' and 'Capri'; with its white pads and slim blue filaments, this is a truly wonderful variety. The plant breeders need to work on a tall version.

Like petunias and geraniums, the best ageratums were once raised from cuttings; a revival is perhaps overdue. This would allow the bicolored style of 'Southern Cross' to be created in other color combinations in a genus that seed breeders find intractable.

LEFT *'Southern Cross' is the best of all the ageratums. Its unique combination of blue and white surges through* Tanacetum parthenium *'White Gem' in a low-level combination which will last for months as long as both plants are regularly deadheaded. Sneaky snips low down on both plants will leave the plants rejuvenated yet not looking butchered.*

Alcea *Hollyhock*

The humble hollyhock is enjoying an exciting revival. The widespread destructiveness of rust disease had led to a dramatic decline in their popularity; now, with the introduction of effective fungicides, gardeners happy to use non-organic methods can again grow good hollyhocks.

The plant breeders have responded. Consistency in the seed-raised doubles such as the Chater's Doubles Series is much improved and 'Powder Puffs', in five pure colors, is an excellent refinement. New shades with winsome names like 'Peaches 'n' Dreams' have been introduced and the mixtures of single-flowered types, usually known simply as 'Single Mixed', have improved their flower forms and the range of colors.

Plant breeders were also tempted – they just can't resist – into creating dwarf hollyhocks to be grown as annuals rather than biennials. The resulting 'Majorette' is an ugly creation that demeans the good name of this classic cottage garden plant. Fortunately, it's disappearing.

Rather than try these monstrosities, try the many heirloom strains which are to found in catalogs: strains like 'Indian Spring', in singles and semi-doubles which date back to the 1930s, and 'Norma Avery' in rose and carmine shades. In addition, there's a much neglected group of hybrids which deserve better attention. *Alcea ficifolia* has leaves shaped like those of a fig, as the name suggests, and the wild form usually has flowers in a pretty primrose shade. This species has two advantages: it's a more consistent perennial than the much more widespread and better developed *A. rosea;* and it is also more resistant to rust.

A number of interesting forms were grown in Eastern Europe including some with ruffled flowers; these have not yet appeared in catalogs for home gardeners. However, from Holland comes a mixture which includes pinks, reds, yellows, and white. This is listed, in the few catalogs which carry it, simply as *A. ficifolia* mixed. I suspect we'll see more of this group in the future.

There are two ways to grow good hollyhocks. Allow them to self-sow in good soil and a sunny site and they develop extensive root systems, their crowns bursting with buds. This works best if you grow just one color; self-sown mixtures are too unpredictable. Hollyhocks can also be raised in pots from a late spring sowing. Prick them out into 3½ in./9 cm. pots and as these fill with roots plant them where they're to flower. If, as is likely, there's no room in your borders in summer, move them on so they finish in 8 in./20 cm. pots; then either plant them in autumn or overwinter them in a cold frame for planting in early spring.

Alcea rosea 'Chater's Double Rose'

OVERLEAF *At Hadspen House in Somerset, southwest England, Nori and Sandra Pope have created the finest color-themed planting in Britain. Here, black hollyhocks,* Alcea rosea *'Nigra', mingle with self-sown seedlings of the dark-leaved orach,* Atriplex hortensis var. rubra. *This valuable foliage plant self-seeds all too generously so most seedlings must be removed; the trick is to leave those which will associate most successfully with neighboring perennials. The reddish magenta of the perennial* Knautia macedonica *in front and the scattering of* Cosmos *'Dazzler' pick up the color in the paler edges of the hollyhock flowers, while the pin k spikes of* Veronica *'Pink Damask' mingling with* Linaria purpurea *'Canon Went' behind add sparks.*

Amaranthus *Amaranthus*

Nowhere else in this book will you find two such contrasting groups of plants under the same heading. United only in their botanical similarities, this likeness is totally overshadowed by their startling, if more superficial, differences and in the scorn in which both groups are commonly held. But this is my plea: don't be too hard on them.

In cooler climates those with tasselled flowers are the more widely grown. Covering a range of species including *Amaranthus caudatus* (known as love-lies-bleeding) and other grain amaranths like *A. hypochondriachus*, *A. cruentus* and *A. paniculatus*, the crowded tassels trail downwards in the first, hence the lies-bleeding common name, and stand up more cheekily in the rest.

A mature plant of the dusty red *A. caudatus*, or its pale green flowered variant var. *viridis*, is a spectacular creature. Its best reaches perhaps 4 ft./1.2 m. and as much across, but only rich soil and no shortage of water produces a specimen of this majestic stature. The waterfall of tassels tumbles to the soil or, better, on to a stone pathway from a narrow border. Plants are best with a wall behind to which the stout stems can be secured; heavy rain can beat them down and, while tying up an annual as if it were a climber may seem unusual, believe me it's necessary.

As specimen plants in a large container with three, perhaps, planted together and supported discreetly on stout canes, the effect is both surprising and impressive, adding an unsuspected grandeur to this sometimes despised plant.

Amaranthus tricolor *'Splendens'*

Amaranthus cruentus *'Golden Giant'*

The tall, dark-leaved and dark-flowered 'Hopi Red Dye', and the uncomfortably similar 'Komo', makes a bold and rather imposing long-season border feature. For many gardeners the shorter and more stiffly upstanding 'Pygmy Torch', crimson in both leaf and flower, and the yellowish green 'Green Thumb' will be more convenient, although the lack of vigor of the dwarf types can lead to their flowering for a relatively short season. Recently a number of new forms has appeared, the 14 ft./2 m. *A. cruentus* 'Golden Giant' is especially useful. Its biscuit-brown, arching tassels hang forward over lower, frontal neighbors like striped, speckled or mahogany-centered yellow *Coreopsis* 'Tiger Stripes' (originally introduced from Arkansas in 1823), and always slightly variable. In rich soil some support may be needed to prevent the plant toppling over as rainwater collects in its densely packed flower heads.

But beware those varieties advertised as mixtures, such as 'Magic Fountains'; check the catalog text carefully. Should you think to plant a large container with a combination of colors, once the range extends beyond green and red plants, with

RIGHT *Adding a sultry light to this red planting, already sparked by the blues of Salvia farinacea 'Strata', 'Hopi Red Dye' is an elegant but rarely grown hybrid amaranthus whose flowering side shoots give it an unusually long season. Dianthus 'Red Feather' flutters daintily around. In the background is a strain of* Nicotiana *'Lime Green', alongside the tall* Salvia splendens *'Rambo', similar to 'Bonfire'.*

ABOVE *The forerunner of the startlingly colorful 'Poinsettia Mixed' and 'Joseph's Coat' amaranthus is this* A. tricolor *which is softer in color, more vigorous and easier to grow. Here the dark markings are picked up by 'Black Night' coleus while defiantly sparking through the center is one of the two most elegant of the celosias for annual plantings, 'Flamingo Purple' (the other is the silvery pink 'Flamingo Feather'). The purple tint to its foliage reinforces the sympathetic coloring.*

their trailing habit, the additional colors will, more often than not, be supplied by plants more upright in growth – creating an unpredictable and perhaps unbalanced display.

All the varieties in this group have one unfortunate characteristic in common, a tendency to shed truly vast quantities of seed in warm conditions – almost all of which seems to germinate. Gravel paths disappear under a carpet of lush green, the slender seed leaves soon giving way to fatter foliage and more vigorous roots; pulling them up brings soil into the gravel mulch . . . soil from which, and into which, weed seeds, not to mention more amaranthus, will germinate. You will have to combine thoughtful and, where necessary, prompt deadheading with timely weed control.

The foliage plant A. *tricolor* is the more universally popular species. Most of its varieties, even the long established 'Splendens' (also known as 'Perfecta'), are positively garish by comparison with the wild form. They can be raised successfully in cool areas if treated as half-hardy annuals, moving them into 5 in./12.5 cm. pots, keeping them growing well then planting out into a container or into rich soil in a sunny and sheltered place. But in a cool and dingy summer they languish.

However, if started well, grown on strongly and planted outside from pots, in warmer areas the 3 ft./90 cm. mass of foliage of 'Joseph's Coat', the most widespread variety, develops a luxuriant yet preposterous blend of scarlet, yellow and green – all on one plant. 'Poinsettia Mixed' looks to be even more outrageous, with three different color forms in the mixture. For color-themed planting, select individual plants in appropriate colors from the mixture as they develop.

The success of these colorful foliage forms depends entirely on the plants being big, bold, lush and luxuriant. In cool areas, they often fail, combining wimpish stature with lurid coloring; such sickly specimens prompt ridicule or, at best, a pitying look from visitors. At their most exuberant they create a real spectacle and provide sharper colorings, to be used sparingly, in tropical summer plantings with bananas, castor beans, solanums, the unique black leaves of 'Palisandra' coleus and other plants reveling in similar conditions.

Antirrhinum *Snapdragon*

Snapdragons are a sad case: so much potential yet the cause of so much disappointment. We should, perhaps, take the Buddhist approach: Buddhists teach (this is a rather curt, nay brutal, paraphrase but you'll get the idea) that suffering is the result of unfulfilled desire and to avoid suffering we should cease desiring. Taking the tortuous ride from there to horticulture . . . if we didn't expect so much of the humble snapdragon we would not be quite so disappointed.

For snapdragons are almost unique among annuals. Plants of real character which also provide a very colorful display, they're in a class of their own compared with African marigolds, impatiens and dumpy little ageratums. They come in three different flower forms, a wide and intriguing range of colors and bicolors, they make good cut flowers and, when planted in herbaceous and mixed borders, actually look as if they belong there. They're tough, they can be raised at lower temperatures than most annuals, they can be planted out without damage before the last spring frosts are over . . . not bad, eh?

The problem is rust. This is a dramatic and devastating disease which can wipe out a whole planting in ten days, often when the plants are at their peak, and for which, unfortunately, there is no cure. Recent research has shown that resistance is controlled by nine separate genes and even if breeders could create a full range of resistant colors (they managed two then gave up) it would be a short time before the rust mutated into a form which could overcome the resistance. Fortunately, modern fungicides will do a good job if used regularly as a preventative spray, if you choose an appropriate brand (not all fungicides are effective against rust). Rust is much easier to prevent than to cure, so don't wait until you see the first pale spots on the tops of the leaves with the corresponding dark rusty marks underneath before spraying.

Recent developments have revealed an interesting transatlantic distinction in attitudes. Until recently, most American introductions have been very dwarf with a tightly rounded, almost flat habit and are very early flowering but lack the long flowering season which most gardeners appreciate. In Europe there has been more interest in reviving old, usually taller varieties – some going back to the nineteenth century – and those with an unusually long flowering season. Gardeners have downplayed those which start to flower exceptionally early then fizzle out in midsummer.

The Chimes Series and the open-throated Bells Series may be colorful, but so what? 'Can be sold in flower in April from a late January sowing', it says in one of the trade catalogs. The natural following sentence 'and will be dead by midsummer' is, not unexpectedly, omitted. The French-bred Kim Series flowers for far longer but starts later – so is largely ignored by suppliers of garden centers in spite of Royal Horticultural Society Awards of Garden Merit for seven out of the nine colors. Frankly, even the best of these dwarf varieties is difficult to use in the garden. The exception is 'Lampion' which is prolific, even elegant, when grown in the ground.

Move up a size, to about 15–18 in./38–45 cm., and a world of possibilities opens. The Sonnet Series provides a splendid range including the

Antirrhinum *'Bells Yellow'*

Antirrhinum *'Brighton Rock'* (single color)

purest of the whites, and it's in this height range that most of the Victorian revivals appear.

The striped snapdragons were a nineteenth-century special – since the Victorians liked almost anything in stripes. Now they're beginning to be relisted as 'Brighton Rock', 'Bizarre' or 'Candyman'; almost all are mixtures which include a small percentage of unstriped plants, a genetic quirk which cannot be eliminated; 'Torbay Rock' is a red-and-yellow available separately, with 50% pure reds – forget it, the blend of stripes and solid red is very uncomfortable. No other separate colors are available. The mixtures are, it has to be said, rather confetti creations. The only way to ensure harmonious plantings is to grow the plants in containers, then select individual plants for specific plantings from their first flowers.

'Black Prince', with its blood red foliage and slightly brighter red flowers, is another old sort which has not been replicated in modern series. With dark-leaved beetroot 'Bull's Blood', and *Dianthus* 'Telstar Crimson' or the even darker, white picoteed 'Velvet 'n' Lace' (also known as 'Black and White Minstrels' and 'Chianti'), plus the sprawling trails of silver-leaved licorice plant, *Helichrysum petiolare*, peeping out where they will, you have a very classy grouping. *Antirrhinum* 'Night and Day', a white-tubed form of 'Black Prince' recently rediscovered in Holland, replicates another Victorian style and would pick up the silver foliage and white picotee of the dianthus. This color combination has now appeared as the open-throated 'La Bella Red and White'.

The other popular shade, apart from white, has long been rose-pink and, among the huge range of separate colors in three or four different heights listed in turn-of-the-century catalogs, rose-pink seems to feature strongly. Pale pinks from the modern Sonnet and Liberty series are noticeably chunky in habit, a result of their

RIGHT *Orange, yellow and rusty colors make a hot and attractive association, here focusing on 'Sonnet Bronze' snapdragon and* Chrysanthemum coronarium *'Primrose Gem'. The slender spikes of* Bulbine annua *peep through behind, with a stray flower of* Salpiglossis *'Chocolate Pot', while the sparky little* Linaria *'Fantasia Yellow', which flowers in as little as six weeks from seed, snuggles in at the front.*

otherwise welcome tendency to produce far more than a single solitary spike at first flowering.

If you need taller varieties then the Rocket Series reaching 3 ft./90 cm. is ideal. Widely available in eight separate colors, these are splendid long-spiked varieties for the middle and back of the border and for cutting they're magnificent. 'Rocket Lemon' and 'Rocket White' are especially valuable; in fact the more I think about them, the more I realize how good these colors are. Even more separate colors are available in snaps developed as greenhouse cut flowers; these are hard to find in catalogs but seem to do well outside, especially if pinched out when about 6 in./15 cm. high. Separate colors of the azalea-flowered 'Madame Butterfly' are also occasionally listed.

For many years I was at a loss to know why anyone would want to grow the open-throated types like 'Madame Butterfly', the dwarf Bells Series and the recent La Bella Series, a companion for Liberty, because one of the main attractions of antirrhinums is the form of their flowers. When that is transformed, sometimes into rather a muddled shape, they lose their appeal. But it's not that simple. With the flower form changed so much, bees are less able to pollinate the flowers successfully. The result is that the individual flowers stay open for longer so the display lasts longer. In 'Madame Butterfly' the flowers are also partially double, with a few extra segments in the throat; I don't like them, but I can see the point.

LEFT *Tall pink snapdragons are not easy to find in catalogs as separate colors but, clearly, it's worth hunting them out. Here 'Yosemite Pink', bred as a greenhouse cut flower but superb outside, stands just above drifts of* Consolida *'White Cloud' and* Nemesia denticulata, *with the pretty dwarf sweet pea 'Cupid' in the foreground. If you pinch this tall and relatively unbranched antirrhinum at planting time, rather than letting it run straight up, it will send out a whole colony of slightly shorter stems.*

RIGHT *Individual half-hardy annuals can often be slipped into a perennial border very effectively. Here, a single plant of* Antirrhinum *'Liberty White' is set in front of hostas alongside autumn sedums, while dark pink dianthus mingle with paler hardy geraniums.*

LEFT *'Black Prince' is one of two Victorian snapdragons never to have quite disappeared from catalogs (the other is 'Rembrandt', an orange and gold bicolor). Here 'Black Prince' snuggles up in front of the modern 'Rocket Yellow', developed as an outdoor cut flower but superb in borders. Blue echium sprawls in from the side with the silvery* Artemisia *'Powis Castle', and the seed heads of the opium poppy stand out boldly against the dark flowers.*

Aquilegia *Columbine*

Still sparking a fond nostalgia among all but the most determinedly progressive gardeners, the traditional cottage-garden columbines have been joined in recent years by a great range of flower forms and color combinations; with the rediscovery of those with colored foliage there's now an almost bewildering choice. There are even varieties to be grown as pot plants. What's more, their innocent promiscuity ensures the garden is swiftly peopled with the unpredictable offspring of the few with which you started.

Most columbines are naturally perennial plants but, because they develop so quickly, growing them as biennials is easy. Invaluable late-spring plants, they provide delightful leaf patterning followed by a long succession of flowers. Raised in pots from an early sowing, rediscovered forms with yellow or yellow-speckled foliage have proved a fine foil for summer flowers.

The first yellow-leaved aquilegia was seen at the Royal Horticultural Society trials of 1914. Called 'Vervaeneana', a name still seen, the difficulty in developing a true stock soon led to its rarity. Now breeders have developed two dependable forms: 'Woodside Variegated Mixed' has mainly mottled foliage with flowers in a wide range of colors; from this came 'Mellow Yellow', with unmottled, soft yellow foliage which flowers

Aquilegia viridiflora

Aquilegia *McKana Group*

Aquilegia vulgaris *Vervaeneana Group*

only in the palest blue and white.

In the rich conditions of a container, 'Mellow Yellow' develops a glowing mound of deep yellow foliage in its first summer – but no flowers. It is superb with the yellow daisies of the neat *Bidens* 'Goldie', the chocolate-colored (and chocolate-scented) flowers of *Cosmos atrosanguineus*, cuphea or the old dwarf striped French marigolds. At the end of the season, the plant can be set out in the garden to flower the following year.

Columbines, of course, are best known for their flowers. Most carry nectar-producing spurs projecting from the back of the flower – sometimes short and stout, sometimes elegantly curved, and maybe in a contrasting color. Varieties with names like 'McKana Giants' and 'Long Spurred Hybrids' all have bright, even multicolored flowers with long spurs. Choose these for the classic cottage combinations of the late-spring or early summer English garden with bearded irises, Oriental poppies, white sweet rocket and lupines.

But the spurless doubles are today's choice. 'Nora Barlow', named for the geneticist granddaughter of Charles Darwin who discovered it in her garden around fifty years ago (although a similar form had been known since the sixteenth century), was urgently sought after for many years yet rarely found. With its dense head of slim petals in

pink, white and pale apple green, its urgent licentiousness led to all manner of variations turning up under the name.

More controlled selection has produced a stable series of colors and combinations, sometimes known as 'Nora Barlow's Relatives'. Sow inside in spring, grow outside in a nursery bed, then transplant in autumn with plenty of soil on the roots for the most spectacular specimens. The gorgeous blue and white 'Adelaide Addison' with its rippled skirt and the deep purple and white 'William Guiness' can be treated in the same way.

The newer 1 ft./30 cm.-high Music Series and the rather taller Songbird Series have their niche as the first columbines which can be grown in windowboxes and small containers without looking silly. Most of these have also been developed to flower in summer from a spring sowing – an interesting, if dubious, achievement. Columbines should be over when summer annuals are at their best.

The dusky *A. viridiflora* is different from all these, being more demure; it's sometimes seen masquerading under such pretentious variety names as 'Chocolate Soldier'. A delicate species, it appreciates a choice place and repays close inspection.

Begonia *Begonia*

The first reaction of most gardeners to begonias is to say that they're difficult to raise from seed. Happily, the seed companies have recognized the problem and cleverly developed a number of ways to help gardeners solve, or perhaps skirt round, the undoubted pitfalls.

It does take a certain crazed optimism to raise begonias from seed in the *traditional* way. Just open the packet and you can see why: is there anything in there at all? Begonia seed is so minute that 5,000 can weigh the same as just one sunflower seed. It is, weight-for-weight, more valuable than gold.

Such tiny seed can be difficult even to get out of the packet. Sowing it evenly is often a matter of chance, and damping off and drought are constant threats. Fortunately, some companies now supply begonia seed in vials from which it's easier to sow evenly; some supply pelleted seed which is much more manageable than natural seed; and more varieties are now available as seedlings and young plants. Unfortunately, it may require persistent detective work to track down seed of the best varieties.

Begonias fall into two unexpectedly different groups: the semperflorens begonias, *Begonia semperflorens* (also known as fibrous-rooted or wax), and the more flamboyant tuberous begonias, *B.* x *tuberhybrida*. Both generally do best with some shade. Semperflorens begonias have small single flowers (seed-raised doubles are coming) in reds, pinks and white with fleshy bronze or bright green leaves. Scarlet, white, and picoteed flowers especially suit bronze leaves; white and rose suit bright green leaves. In recent years plant breeders have made them all increasingly tight and inhibited in habit.

And so many are so very similar; most are too small for growing in open borders. The Stara Series is much less compact but the leaves are large and coarse; better, but less often seen, are the noticeably taller and more open Thousand Wonders Series, and the All Round Series which is more vigorous and spreading in growth. Both come in fewer leaf/flower color combinations than smaller types.

In containers where the conditions are richer, generous feeding and constant watering will make even the smaller semperflorens begonias more acceptable; with good living they grow larger and more open in habit. The Victory Series comes in a total of eight colors, both green- and bronze-leaved; the slightly larger-flowered, bronze-leaved Vision Series, in five.

The picotee types are outstanding, especially when combined with bronze foliage. 'Coco Ducolor' was the old favorite and, if you can find it, develops a more open habit than the modern 'Malaga Bicolor' – although when I grew a single plant of the latter in a terra-cotta pot and fed and watered it well, it did look very fine. These bicolors are delightful, but rarely listed.

Tuberous begonias are bolder – positively spectacular compared with semperflorens

Begonia semperflorens 'Victory White'

Begonia semperflorens 'Victory Pink'

RIGHT *Picotee semperflorens begonias are the most attractive of them all; even filling a container without companions they look good. Here, it's 'Coco Ducolor', but any of the admittedly hard-to-find dark-leaved picotees will fit. Silver Senecio cinerarea 'Silver Dust' and a dainty blue viola have been added to create a richer blend; the pink and white Nicotiana 'Havana Appleblossom' would be a more suitable taller neighbor than the lime green.*

Begonia x tuberhybrida *'Happy End'*

ABOVE *Bronze-leaved scarlet begonias make a good specimen display for small spaces. Here, they're enhanced by their dark container and the backing of grassy foliage, which provides contrast in both color and form.*

sorts. Their flowers are huge, almost always fully double, and yet they have so many orange and yellow shades in addition to the reds, pinks, and white seen in semperflorens types, that they make an altogether more uncomfortable mixture. Look for single colors. Most have green leaves, but search out those with bronze foliage and orange, apricot, or scarlet flowers.

'Nonstop' is the big name, but not necessarily the best. Most varieties are too neat and bushy; with one exception, it is the trailing types that stand out. The exception is 'Pin-up'; its large, red-edged, pure-white single flowers make this a fine plant for containers where it will softly call the attention of dreamy passers-by. If you prefer visitors to faint clean away, 'Pin-up Flame', a red and yellow version, should do the job.

In baskets, boxes, and large containers the trailing types are superb; they're vigorous, bold, yet not so chunky and solid as to be totally smothering. 'Happy End' has relatively small, double and semi-double flowers in four colors and a determinedly trailing habit. It works well in a basket by itself. The Illumination Series in a similar habit comes in separate colors; the apricot with its orange buds looks especially good with *Helichrysum petiolare* 'Limelight' licorice plant.

The Panorama Series is less insistently trailing in habit and has the extra benefit of deep bronze or bronze-veined leaves in some colors. This is the most adaptable of all varieties, suiting both baskets and raised, lumber-edged garden beds. The pastel Show Angels Series is a little more lax and a little less uniform in its doubling and in color but, at their best, the flowers are fully double with contrasting picotee edges.

Some tuberous begonias are available as tubers, but many, in both groups, come only as seed. Check the general advice on page 175 but buy pelleted seeds if possible. Don't firm the potting mix, sow seed as evenly as you can, and don't sieve mix over it until after germination. If you have shaky hands or poor eyesight get someone else to do the job. Cover the pot with plastic wrap; keep it at 70°F/21°C out of direct sun. Never let the seeds or seedlings dry out and be sure to treat them against damping off disease.

Bellis English Daisy

"English Daisy" – sounds so quaint and old-fashioned, doesn't it? Well, these dainty winter and spring bloomers have come a long way from their origins in the sheep-nibbled turf of the English hillsides. They've come into lawns, but they've also come into our containers and borders in far more refined forms. All are derived from the little English lawn daisy.

Cultivated forms, especially doubles, have been known since at least the seventeenth century. The early herbalist, John Parkinson, in his *Paradisus Terrestris* of 1629, illustrates some fully double sorts which, even allowing for the usual artistic over-enthusiasm, are very striking. He also features a double hen-and-chickens form which appears to be extinct; only the single-flowered 'Prolifera' remains. These and the more modern double daisies collected by the English garden innovator Margery Fish from cottage gardeners, are all propagated by division but virus infection has, unfortunately, weakened them, making them less easy to propagate.

But seed-raised bellis have improved greatly in recent years. Plants are more prolific, the flowers are more fully double, they last longer before revealing their yellow eye, and are also a little more uniform in their coloring. Like dahlias, the genetic makeup of bellis is unusually complicated, and creating varieties in uniform colors is more difficult than in most plants – though this is not necessarily a disadvantage. What can be disappointing is that, although in warm zones English daisies may flower all through the winter, in cold areas flowering may be restricted to a brief spring flourish.

Bellis can be divided into two groups: large-flowered sorts producing relatively few flowers, and the more prolific small-flowered types. Large-flowered varieties – with names like 'Monstrosa' and 'Goliath' – are big, blowsy, and not at all elegant. They also age disgracefully, eventually revealing a garish yellow eye as the petals curl back and become ragged. Some, though, are more than acceptable. The new, award-winning 'Robella' is an attractive one-of-a-kind, whose large flowers last well before the yellow eye finally appears.

The uniquely colored Habanera Series is an exciting development. The white is pure white but the other three shades are all bicolors. 'Habanera Rose' is white with the petal tips stained pink; 'Habanera Lipstick' (also known as 'Habanera White with Red Tips') has more of the petals stained, this time in bright red; in 'Habanera Red' almost the full length of each petal is bright red, with just a little white at the base. The four colors combine unusually well in the mixture but the chunky flowers of *Tulipa griegii* or *T. kauffmaniana* best balance the impact of the large daisies.

Of the smaller-flowered types, 'Galaxy' can be ruled out at once; the flowers open with a yellow eye which looks especially unpleasant in the pink form. The rest are all highly engaging. Some, like 'Pomponette', have quilled petals creating tight button-like flowers; 'Carpet' has flat petals. Reaching little more than 6 in./15 cm., all these are excellent in containers with dwarf bulbs like muscari or small daffodils; choose the colors carefully.

'Carpet Pink' looks lovely with the white form of *Muscari azureum*. Its color varies slightly and a few plants usually feature white petals tinted red on the backs; the overall effect is pinkish but look closer and it's clear that, as the tissue of each petal becomes thinner towards the edge, the red from the backs shows through. What's more, in the center of the flower the petals roll inwards showing off their red coloring.

Bellis perennis *'Robella'*

LEFT *This delicate spring planting shows that biennials can be used to create the sort of satisfying tapestry which snobbish plantspeople believe is only possible with esoteric woodland flowers from China. With 'Primrose Monarch' wallflower behind, Bellis 'Pomponette White' has been slipped in alongside Milium effusum 'Aureum', Bowles' golden grass. This too is grown as a biennial, but there is rarely a need to do anything but lift it in the fall from where it has self-sown and slide it in where it will look best.*

Brachyscome *Swan River Daisy*

That 's' in *Brachyscome* never used to be there; where did it come from? Now people think you're crazy if you leave it in. The botanist Cassini, who coined the name in 1816, first called them all *Brachyscome* but by 1825 had changed his mind and was calling them *Brachycome*. His second choice became widely used but the original is correct.

Swan River daisies, as they are less confusingly known (the Swan River is in Western Australia), have seen much improvement recently. They've not lost their fresh-mown-hay fragrance, but their habit has become less straggly and unstable without becoming excessively dumpy (the ultimate misdemeanor) and the colors are fresher, clearer and more diverse.

Once there was only purple and a range of watery tones. Then the disappearing 'Summer Skies' added some deeper colors and white, together with some pretty and distinct blue- and lilac-tinted whites. 'Bravo' refined them in a different way: it comes in four clear colors (dark blue, pale blue, violet, and white) each with either a black or a white eye.

Brachyscomes are relatively hardy (they can even be sown outside in many areas), they grow strongly, and are usually in flower at planting time. So you can choose from the eight colors of 'Bravo' or the slightly less predictable, but more subtle shades of 'Summer Skies'.

The white with a black eye could go in a black-and-white planting with *Nemophila* 'Pennie Black', also known as 'Total Eclipse', *Dianthus* 'Black and White Minstrels', and the white 'Giant Hyacinth Flowered' candytuft. In a container or small, richly fed bed the pale blue with a white eye could go with *Petunia* 'Fantasy Sky Blue' in a similar shade.

The blue forms are invaluable in blue-and-white plantings. 'Blue Star' or both the pale and the dark blue from the Bravo Series could merge into *Ageratum* 'Blue Horizon' or the bicolored 'Southern Cross'; their finely cut, fresh green foliage would contrast well with the dark and lustrous leaves of 'Marine' heliotrope. *Salvia farinacea* 'Victoria' would make a harmonious presence in the background while in the front alongside the brachyscome, *Nemesia* 'KLM' would start bright, then fade away as the season advanced, its space to be occupied by the brachyscome and the heliotrope.

LEFT *Using dark-flowered brachyscome with the silver-leaved Senecio cineraria 'Silver Dust' is a familiar yet effective combination, and the white ring in some of the brachyscome flowers, especially those of the older varieties with their narrow petals, creates both harmony and contrast at the same time. In the background is the seed-raised 'Marine' heliotrope, less highly scented than cuttings-raised types, but more prolific.*

Brassica Cabbage and Kale

Goodness, how the humble cabbage and kale have come up in the world. Even people who should know better still scoff at the idea of including cabbages or Brussels sprouts in ornamental plantings; please, ignore these skeptics. Brassicas are among the best of all foliage annuals, and not just those developed exclusively for their supposedly ornamental qualities.

"Ornamental" cabbages and kales should be used with discretion. Often, thoughtful reflection (or, indeed, the more common knee-jerk reaction) will lead you to eschew some of them altogether. No one wants a garden replication of those entrances to industrial parks, edged with the flat heads of ornamental kales in pink, white and green, like the introduction to some bizarre commemorative exhibition of tacky tableware. Individual plants carefully chosen for color – that's very different.

Those bred for their colored foliage are not for summer schemes. Their color develops best as temperatures decrease so they should be sown in most areas in early summer and planted in late summer for brightening the fall garden or even the winter garden. Varieties developed for their culinary use are generally more effective as summer ornamentals, except perhaps in the warmest zones.

Conventional red cabbage, with the smoky blue cast to its leaves, is a fine summer foliage plant and looks superb with blue or pink petunias or *Chrysanthemum segetum* 'Prado'. The older, heirloom open-pollinated types like 'Meteor' are better than modern F_1 hybrids; the newest varieties tend to have few outer leaves yet it's this outer foliage which is the most effective ornamentally.

Red Brussels sprouts like 'Ruby' or

Brassica 'Red Peacock' with Colchicum speciosum

especially the newcomer 'Falstaff' are ideal for a bolder statement if you can find seed, although they may need staking. With trails of canary vine or the silky blue of morning glory 'Heavenly Blue' scrambling among them and producing a constant succession of flowers, they spark both joy and surprise.

Two recently introduced kales are outstanding ornamental foliage plants. 'Redbor' is a cold hardy yet summer sumptuous dark purple-leaved curly kale. It's splendid in combinations with the sharper purple of *Verbena* 'Homestead Purple', a blue-bracted *Salvia viridis*, the slender purple-blue spikes of *Salvia farinacea* 'Victoria' or even scarlet 'Bonfire' salvias. *Petunia* 'Purple Wave', which will scramble through given a little encouragement, makes a startling companion.

The heirloom 'Lacinato', also known as 'Nero di Toscana', is quite different but no less striking. Originally a traditional Italian variety, sometimes known as 'Black Tuscany', its more open habit allows neighbors such as the gray-leaved *Eucalyptus globulus* or magenta petunias to sneak their stems in among its long, rumpled blue-green foliage, creating a wild blend of associations.

These summer brassicas appreciate root space in the early stages. Sown in early to mid-spring, then pricked out into 3½ in./9 cm. and then 5 in./12.5 cm. pots they should have enough room to develop without the combined risk of drought and starvation which will prompt the lower leaves to drop.

Once you plant brassicas, cabbage whitefly, flea beetle, and caterpillars can cause trouble, but the latter two seem less of a problem on 'Redbor' than on all the others.

ABOVE *The Black Tuscan kale, often known as 'Lacinato', may not actually be black but it's surely one of the most impressive foliage plants for summer bedding. Here, the aptly named, cuttings-raised Verbena 'Snowflurries' mingles with it, creating a bold contrast, with Nemesia denticulata and the foliage of a black coleus filling in the background.*

ABOVE *Vegetables can be beautiful too. In front, the curly red kale 'Redbor' makes foaming mounds of lava-like foliage which is impressive from planting time right through to the following spring in most areas. At the back, the chunky blue-green fountains of 'Lacinato' stand out boldly among the blue ageratums, petunias, and morning glories which tie the display together, sparked by white spikes of Salvia farinacea 'Cirrus'.*

Calendula *Pot Marigold*

Since the first years of settlement this dazzling annual has brightened American gardens. Used as an antiseptic by the original settlers, the Shakers found it indispensable in preventing gangrene. More recently its flowers have sparkled in the salads of fashionable restaurants and herb gardens all over the country.

Originally, calendulas were tall, open and with single flowers in bright orange-yellow. Now breeders have broadened their colors, developed their flower forms, and reduced their height. Unfortunately, little has been achieved in the continuing battle against powdery mildew. And this is one of the two reasons why the very dwarf calendulas like 'Fiesta Gitana' are unsatisfactory; the other, of course, is that they can be so very ugly. Their congested growth restricts air circulation among the plants with the result that, although they were selected with mildew resistance in mind, the disease prospers in such close conditions, often disfiguring plants in their prime. The overcrowding of stems and foliage also prevents thorough spraying – so mildew is almost guaranteed.

However, in their taller forms, calendulas are both invaluable and consistently endearing. They bring a color range similar to that of African and French marigolds but with no tendency to the grossness of the former or the unnatural congested dumpiness of the latter. The introduction of a small number of more pastel, even pinkish,

Calendula *'Double Lemon Coronet'*

tones increases their versatility. Their habit is another feature that marks them out. They have a natural angularity of growth and a branching habit, both of which prevent all the flowers from being held in a flat plane at the top of the plant; this not only makes them easy to deadhead but leaves the deadheaded plants looking as if they never needed attention in the first place.

In annual borders, calendulas generally occupy the middle ground. Although the subtle coloring of varieties like 'Indian Prince' and 'Touch of Red' with chestnut or mahogany backs to the petals is best appreciated close up, it's inevitable that the lower parts of the plant become a little ragged. They need a place where slightly shorter plants like blue echiums, bronze-leaved *Hibiscus acetosella* or dark-eyed *Cosmidium* (*Thelesperma*) 'Brunette' can effect clever coverups.

Calendula *'Kablouna'*

Calendula *'Touch of Red'*

In mild areas, calendulas are at their best in winter and spring; even in less favored regions they may fade in the heat of midsummer. However, in cool conditions they are especially good grown as specimens or groups in autumn borders where dark-leaved asters, particularly forms of *Aster lateriflorus* such as 'Prince' and 'Horizontalis', can hide those bare stems with their sympathetic coloring, then take center stage as the calendulas finally fade. Asters also help with support.

As with so many members of the daisy family, calendulas

RIGHT *Sultry red, orange, yellow and gold make an unbeatable combination of colors. This all-dark selection from the bicolored Coreopsis 'T&M Originals Mixed' is about to be overwhelmed by nasturtium 'Forest Flame', which will need to be kept in order to prevent it from taking over the whole flower bed. Calendula 'Indian Prince', the backs of whose petals echo the color of the coreopsis, also connects with Rudbeckia 'Toto' in the front. The rich olive foliage belongs to Haloragis 'Melton Bronze', an invaluable new foliage plant related, believe it or not, to gunnera!*

show intriguing variations in the form of their flowers. The delicate simplicity of the wild single-flowered types may be essential in annual meadows. By contrast, the unexpected sophistication of the anemone-centered Kablouna Series is delightful and it makes an invaluable cut flower; unfortunately it is also difficult for the seed grower to keep the plant true to type.

From the radiant, perhaps impossibly garish, cactus-bloomed 'Radio' (great with *Dahlia* 'David Howard') to the variable 'Pacific Mixed', the full doubles are the most familiar, but all eventually open to reveal the eye of the flower; the more fully double, the longer it takes – but keeping them fully double takes the seed grower time. So the most reliable seed for doubles is likely to be the most expensive.

Almost every year, individual colors from one series or another, such as 'Double Lemon Coronet' or one-of-a-kinds like 'Campfire', are released. Many of these are very beautiful, either in the purity of their pale shades or the delicacy of their bicolors. But frankly, they tend to be transient, so those you enjoy one year may vanish from catalogs the next. Mixtures, like the old 'Art Shades' and 'Pacific Mixed', and the more recent Kablouna-style 'Buttercreams Mixed', often include colors rarely seen separately, but the quality and uniformity may vary between suppliers.

All the double forms make excellent cut flowers. The stems may not be long but the individuality of the flowers can at least be enjoyed in small arrangements. Cut them just before the flowers are fully open, plunge them immediately into water, then remove the leaves and recut before arranging them.

Seeds of calendulas are intriguingly curved and bristly, and sufficiently large to be easily sown by hand where they're to flower. Space them widely from the start and thin quickly so that they branch. Although calendulas often behave as winter annuals in the wild, in gardens the soil may be too heavy and the season too wet and/or cold – so the survival rate can be poor. You can move seedlings without too much disruption in spring, but for more careful positioning it's better to sow calendulas in cool conditions (a cold frame or cold greenhouse rather than a heated propagator), pricking them out into trays, then individual 3 in./7 cm. pots, and plant before the roots become crowded.

LEFT *Two hardy annuals, calendula and borage, both with a naturally open habit, mingle contentedly. The white form of borage, Borago officinalis 'Alba', will soon be as widely grown as the blue form – it self-sows as enthusiastically and often needs thinning out. Calendulas self-sow too and, unless carefully rogued, lose their double flowers in favor of the more natural single forms of their wild ancestors.*

Callistephus *China Aster*

There's something warming and uniquely comforting about China asters. Perhaps it's the softness in the coloring of their end-of-season flowers, a dull glow which, throughout the color range – a range wider than that of most annuals – allows a mellowing of any potential harshness. And their fixed place as late-season flowers, gently marking the end of summer, looking back on a brighter season, on the brink of a chillier change . . . it all fits with the nostalgic mood.

But sales of China asters were fading for years, even for decades. Gardeners developed a taste for brighter flowers and, at the same time, the increase in aster wilt disease ensured that China asters were often unsuccessful, especially in small gardens. The wilt problem is still with us; trials have proved that there are no wilt-resistant asters – whatever the catalogs say. But the softness of their coloring does now have a stronger appeal to modern gardeners. And their long, wiry stems keep them a favorite for cutting.

Taller and medium-sized China asters fit well into mixed borders. Forget the shortest types, like the appalling 'Starlight Rose' which, at about 6 in./ 15 cm., flowers in a single brief burst before it shrivels. The medium and taller callistephus are splendid companions for perennial asters, late pokers, sedums, grasses, and other autumn perennials.

'Florette Champagne', reaching about 2 ft./60 cm., is a gorgeous soft champagne shade with a touch of pink in its long slender petals; set it amid the dark stems of *Aster lateriflorus* 'Prince'. 'Opus', in cream with pink tips, could go behind rustier pink autumn sedums and a dwarf blue perennial aster like 'Professor Anton Kippenberg'. The 'Prinette' mix-

ture with pale centered flowers and needle-like petals is a prolific blend of richer shades; the restricted color mix allows it to be used in perennial borders where broader mixtures could jar.

Separate colors in China asters are available from a few catalogs. Mixtures prevail, although this is fine if you grow them for cutting; cut just as the flowers are opening and be sure to remove the lower leaves. The frilly ostrich-plume style 'Crego Finest Mixed', the crested-flowered 'Giant Princess Mixed' in an amazing 17 colors, and 'Duchess' with flowers like incurved chrysanthemums, are all worth growing. But the color blend may vary with the supplier, so if you feel you have too few colors, try the same variety from another supplier the following year.

The Modern Japanese types, like the Matsumoto Series, are different. These are bred for upright growth and to branch well from the base so that, instead of cutting single stems, the whole plant is cut just above soil level: one plant makes a bouquet. Don't be afraid to do exactly that.

Aster wilt remains a problem. Wilt is a soil-borne disease and growing China asters in the same place two years running is a mistake. To avoid attack, plant China asters in a different space in the border each year or, if you grow them for cutting, rotate them around the vegetable plot or cutting garden. To grow a few for cutting in infected soil, plant them out from 5 in./12.5 cm. pots to provide each plant with a kernel of wilt-free soil.

It's also worth remembering that China asters are unhappy in acid soil. Adding lime to bring the soil pH up to at least neutral will make for healthy plants which are less likely to succumb to wilt.

Callistephus chinensis *'Prinette Mixed'*

LEFT *The original wild form of* Callistephus chinensis *is a simple and elegant plant. In naturalistic plantings it's far more sympathetic in form than more highly bred type, which are often too bold or blowsy. Here, with the neat seed-heads of baby's breath,* Gypsophila elegans, *it makes an attractive late-season combination. Single California Giant China asters, in a wide range of colors and bicolors but with simple single flowers, are similar in style to the wild species but the addition of so many extra shades brings extra variety to naturalistic plantings.*

Campanula *Bellflower*

How, as they say, are the mighty fallen. In the days of the great English manor houses biennial campanulas were a crucial and spectacular element in staged indoor displays. *Campanula pyramidalis* was the main choice, and was even known as the chimney bellflower from its most frequent position in the house in summer. Now it's rarely grown, either here or in England, but still worthwhile outdoors as a border biennial in milder areas where its vast quantities of smaller flowers are often less combative in appearance than the chunkier bells of *C. medium*. In cold areas and heavy soils it may not survive the winter.

The Canterbury bell, *C. medium*, also has a history as a display plant for the grand country houses and, given large pots and rich feeding, can be truly spectacular – as well as long lasting. Sown in early spring, moved on so plants never become potbound, kept cool while they're indoors, and fed – well, they can be astonishing. These days, it's easier to prick them out into 3½ in./9 cm. pots, line them in a row in the garden, then move them to their flowering places in autumn.

Their natural form is the simple bell, in blue, pink, or white. The cup-and-saucer forms, with their enlarged and colored calyx, are more dramatic and altogether more colorful, but they can be too overpowering alongside more demure neighbors in mixed borders. Semi-double forms are also sometimes listed. All tend to be named descriptively: 'Cup and Saucer Mixed', 'Double Mixed', and so on. For containers and for smaller gardens, 'Ring of Bells' is a dwarf, 15 in./38 cm., cup-and-saucer type in the usual colors plus lilac; 'Bells of Holland' is a slightly taller, bell-flowered equivalent, also in four colors, at about 18 in./45 cm. Most unexpected is 'Russian Pink', at 15–18 in./38–45 cm, which can be grown as a half-hardy annual or a biennial and comes only in this soft rose shade. It is said to flower in just 16 weeks from a spring sowing. A better show from more elegant plants comes from overwintering. This makes a splendid container plant.

The dainty *C. patula* on its wiry stems is registering an upsurge of interest and is certainly the pick for most gardeners, although seed remains difficult to find in catalogs.

Campanula medium *'Single Rose Pink'*

The seed-raised forms of *C. carpatica*, in blue and in white, are valuable in containers. This is an underrated biennial, unusual in combining neat growth with a poise uncommon in dwarf varieties. Grow 'Blue Clips' with dwarf daffodils like *Narcissus* 'Tête à Tête', or in both colors with *Muscari azureum* or *M. botryoides* in the same two shades.

Summer-flowering *C. isophylla* had a few heady years as a popular trailer for summer containers, raised as a half-hardy annual; however, its brittle growth habit has relegated it not quite to the obscurity from whence it came, but it's now less easy to find. The Stella Series is the one to look for, but it needs an early sowing to flower from July.

LEFT *Canterbury bells have traditionally been grown as specimens for indoor decoration, for greenhouse display, as bold displays in cottage gardens, and sometimes in large pots by the door. More frequently, now, they're slipped into mixed plantings, as here with white violets. The 'Bells of Holland' mixture reaches only about 18 in./45 cm. in height, ensuring that this approach is more manageable in smaller gardens.*

ABOVE *The smaller campanulas are much underused spring container plants, bringing both color and character to what can be predictable displays. Planted in spring from plants in flower, or almost so, 'White Clips' and 'Blue Clips', both seed-raised forms of* Campanula carpatica, *snuggle up to* Primula *'Wanda Supreme Blue',* Anemone blanda *'Atrocaerulea', boldly splashed variegated ivy, and white hyacinth 'L'Innocence'.*

ABOVE *The delicacy of the British native* Campanula patula, *a rare biennial, is perfect here, where it has sown itself into a gap between plants of* Alchemilla mollis *in its clouds of pale green foam. The only problem with this delightful combination is that when the time comes to cut back the alchemilla to prevent it throwing sheets of self-sown seedlings, the campanula may also be cut down when its seedlings would be valuable.*

Centaurea *Bachelor's Button*

In a country settled by people who left their places of birth, enduring hardship, not only on the hazardous journey across the ocean, but in making a life in a new country, nostalgic connections with home run deep. The settlers brought seeds of their favorite flowers to remind them of home and family but some seeds arrived by accident in the grain they brought to sow.

Bachelor's button, *Centaurea cyanus*, also known as cornflower, was a common weed of wheatfields in Europe and, with poppies and other annual flowers, brightened the colonist's first harvests in the new country. Its sparks of blue were taken into gardens from the fields, then cut for simple windowsill displays.

Both here and in Europe variants in pink and white appeared and the bachelor's button came to the attention of plant breeders who worked in two directions. They reduced its height and developed its bushiness to create a more acceptable bedding plant, and they also increased its color range and basal branching to enhance its potential as a cut flower – and as a border plant.

The Midget Series is simply too small and squat to be taken seriously but the Florence Series, at about 12–14 in./30–35 cm. and in six colors, five of which are Fleuroselect Award winners, is quite something. The plants are impressively prolific; sometimes the heads of the plants are almost too packed with flowers but no more so, I suppose, than a dwarf Michaelmas daisy. The Florence Series flower for a long season and snipping a few shoots for small bouquets goes entirely unnoticed. However, they make such dense plants that pugnacious companions are needed to break them into less solid blocks. *Helichrysum petiolare* again comes to the rescue, its silver shoots insistently surging through; they look especially comfortable in 'Florence Lavender' and 'Florence Pink'.

There are some interesting forms in taller bachelor's buttons. The 'Frosted Queen' mixture, whose white petal-tips create an altogether lighter look, sparkles against dark-leaved shrubs like the deep purple-leaved *Cotinus coggygria* 'Royal Red', even in the full mixture of blues, purples and pinks. Separate colors are not available in the 'Frosted Queen' type but the Boy Series of tall varieties for cutting, for the back of annual borders and for mixed borders, now comes separately in black (in truth, more of a deep rich purple), white (sometimes called 'Snowman'), red, and the usual cornflower blue. I suspect this is the same as the Ball Strain sometimes listed.

LEFT *Blue may be an uncommon color in hardy annuals but these three species from a blue-themed hardy annual mix make a sparkling combination. The deep blue California native, desert bluebells,* Phacelia campanularia, *is one of the quickest hardy annuals to flower and later gives way to other varieties. The wild bachelor's button,* Centaurea cyanus, *continues to flower as the weeks pass, while another western native, the softer* Nemophila menziesii *with its white eye has a long season unless allowed to become dry.*

Here is a case where the setting is crucial, for these are tall plants that can be lost, highlighted, or made partners by their background. 'Black Boy', against silver *Elaeagnus angustifolia*, stands out well – in fact the result is truly beautiful; against a purple beech hedge the effect is entirely different, but as impressive in a heavy, sultry sort of way; but against a cherry laurel hedge, *Prunus laurocerasus*, the light and shade of the cherry laurel's large leathery leaves detract from the bachelor's button more gentle display.

'Snowman' works against the same two backgrounds for the opposite reasons: against the elaeagnus it harmonizes, against the beech it stands out brightly; 'Red Ball' looks superb against the fresh green of an arborvitae hedge; 'Blue Ball', sown a little late and set in gaps in a late summer and autumn border, provides electric sparks among crocosmias and red-hot pokers against a dark yew hedge.

All these taller types are best planted from pots, the better to allow their roots to develop and to allow them to become substantial plants before being set among permanent plants which would overwhelm smaller specimens.

Mildew can sometimes cause problems in dry summers, although the congested growth of the Florence Series seems unexpectedly, though not totally, resistant. Spraying against mildew, deadheading, and cutting for the house have a noticeably beneficial effect on staying power.

Taller types require support. Branching as they do, simply looping string around the clump usually proves unsatisfactory: the plants lean more and more heavily over the string. Stretching 6 in./15 cm. mesh netting horizontally between canes, at about 18 in./45 cm. above ground, supports the stems more effectively.

RIGHT *The spreading growth of* Geranium x riversleaianum *'Mavis Simpson' sprawls among the tall shoots of 'Black Boy' bachelor's buttons, which are flopping adrift from their supports, with occasional shoots of the white-tipped* Salvia viridis *'Claryssa White' peeping through. The geranium spreads so much that it requires wide spacing, but well-established plants of the bachelor's button and salvia can be set into this space to grow away and not be overwhelmed by the tide of geranium growth.*

Cerinthe *Honeywort*

I've lost count of the number of times I've read that cerinthes grow wild in New Zealand. Where this nonsense came from I cannot imagine, but nonsense it is. Cerinthes are annuals or short-lived perennials which originate in southern Europe and can be seen by tourists taking a spring vacation in the Mediterranean. This also gives you some indication of the conditions honeyworts prefer in gardens.

Cerinthe major var. *purpurascens* is the one which has taken plant lovers by the scruff and demanded to be grown in their gardens. In addition to its entirely unexpected blue-purple coloring it has the great benefit of often lasting through the winter in many areas – well, through one winter at least. 'Kiwi Blue' looks very similar – named because the seed was originally sent to Britain from a gardener in New Zealand, not because it grows there in the wild.

Spring-sown plants will flower among blue agapanthus; a dusting of white baby's breath is a glittery companion. Overwintered plants will flower with irises; with the almost outrageous blue-tinted black 'Dusky Challenger', they are simply astonishing.

But there are others. *Cerinthe major* itself has brown-tipped yellow flowers with noticeable, white spotted leaves. This is the more typical Mediterranean form and it

Cerinthe major *var.* purpurascens

is a wonderful, autumn-germinating, dry garden plant. The young leaves are long, rounded, and pale and distinctively spotted in white. Then, provided they are given the space, the young plants will naturally branch well from the base, developing relatively few stout branches as they mature. The flowers hang, partially hidden by bracts, from arching spikes, so plants are best sown, or allowed to remain, near a path where the flowers can be examined close up.

The yellow-flowered *C. minor* is exactly that – minor – but best of all is the stunning *C. retorta*, which is bold enough to make an impact from a distance. My seed was sent out of the blue, having been collected, with permission I might add, from the garden of the British Embassy in Athens. This is another winter annual; the bracts around the flower, bluish in *C. major* var. *purpurascens*, in *C. retorta* are deep purple.

Seed of all three plants tends to be relatively short-lived (and in short supply), but the large nutlets can be collected from the base of the flowering stems while the topmost flowers are still open. Sow them at once, or simply allow the plants to self-sow – which they will do readily on gravel in a sunny place in many zones; in the hotter areas, a position in part-shade is more suitable.

Chrysanthemum *Annual Chrysanthemum*

It's a relief to realize that these innocent yet exciting Mediterranean chrysanthemums have so little in common with the cheerleader's pompons seen on show benches. So little, in fact, that botanists have given those we grow as annuals not one but five genera all to themselves (see page 184). For, while those show chrysanthemums may be truly remarkable, they're as distant from anyone's idea of a companionable garden plant as a prickly pear cactus. And while the show bench chrysanthemums are known (and loved or despised) for their size and perfection of form, annual chrysanthemums boast other qualities more suited to the garden: adaptability and sparklingly original color.

Color in annual chrysanthemums is unique in two ways. There's a purity in the buttercup color of wild *C. coronarium* – and in its pale semi-double form, 'Primrose Gem' – which is rare and refreshing. 'Primrose Gem' brings out the richness in *Salpiglossis* 'Chocolate Pot' and the coppery undertow of Snapdragon 'Sonnet Bronze'.

In the wild, the pure buttercup yellow is the dominant form, but in many areas there's a small, more or less constant, proportion of a yellow-eyed white form, var. *discolor*. This persists in gardens, creating occasional refreshing surprises, as in the wild.

In C. *carinatum*, purity of color is just one attraction – and the purity is by no means universal. Muddy shades have crept in, but it's still the sparkling color combinations which are so surprising, so exhilarating. However, now that we're mostly reduced to 'Court Jesters', 'Merry Mix', and similar fling-all-the-colors-in-

together type mixtures, hunting out separate colors like the very clean 'Polar Star' and the newer red-and-yellow bicolored 'German Flag' is proving more difficult. But more of these single colors are coming.

Like so many bicolored flowers, the colors of 'Polar Star' make valuable links with neighbors. The dark eye connects with the foliage of *Hibiscus acetosella* 'Red Shield'; the yellow ring could be picked up in 'Sonnet Yellow' snapdragons, and the white in silver foliage or *Lavatera* 'White Cherub'; trained on a fence or wigwam of canes behind, the lemon and white climber *Mina lobata* 'Citronella' would pick up both colors.

Chrysanthemum coronarium *'Primrose Gem'*

Chrysanthemum carinatum *'Polar Star'*

There are also doubles, daintier and altogether more interesting than the more familiar double florist's chrysanthemums – or rather, there were. Usually seen under the name of 'Dunnettii', these are now hardly listed in catalogs, although they were once available in separate colors. When the doubles are derived from forms with ray florets in two or three bands of color, the result can be delightful. Unfortunately, the doubles are even more rare than the name 'Dunnettii', for this name is sometimes now used to cover an unpredictable blend of both singles and doubles.

There are two other annual chrysanthemums which demand attention. The corn marigold, C. *segetum*, was once a familiar cornfield weed in Europe but has declined dramatically since herbicide use became so common. This species is a useful and long-flowering garden plant, while 'Prado', with black-centered bright yellow flowers, is the

LEFT *This sharp yellow planting features close harmony in the flower colors and basic flower form, with just enough contrast in the other aspects to make it interesting. The naturally dwarf sunflower 'Pacino', with its slightly ragged ring of petals, is surrounded by the contrastingly finely cut foliage of a wild-collected* Chrysanthemum cornarium *from the Greek islands. In front, a not-very-rustic example of* Rudbeckia *'Rustic Dwarfs' is infiltrated with* Bidens *'Golden Eye', also with dissected foliage, and the yellow-edged leaves of* Pelargonium *'Charity'.*

form most often listed. Adding 'Black Prince' snapdragon and *C. multicaule* around the base makes a bold grouping. The lower, looser habit of *C. multicaule* enables it to sprawl around the base of taller plants, and under African marigolds it successfully tones down their brashness. 'Gold Plate', in bright butter yellow, and the paler 'Moonlight' are the most readily available; there's rumored to be a white.

The two most widely grown chrysanthemum species, namely *C. carinatum* (tricolor chrysanthemum) and *C. coronarium* (crown daisy), both originate in Mediterranean regions. One of the most obvious aspects of the way that annuals adapt to the native Mediterranean climate is that most germinate in late summer and autumn. They then develop as the temperature cools and the rainfall rises, continuing to grow throughout the winter and making an extensive root system which then sustains the plants as the temperature rises again and rainfall drops off in spring.

Plants which are well established when temperatures rise will continue to grow, making larger and more impressive plants and flowering for many weeks even in high temperatures. In addition to chrysanthemums many other native Mediterranean annuals, including poppies and larkspur, behave in this way. We replicate this adaptation in the garden by sowing in autumn.

However, away from the moist, mild winters of the Mediterranean and similar climates, colder, wetter winters combined with a heavy soil reduces the chances of overwintering. Sowing indoors in early spring, growing cool and potting on before the pots become crowded with roots is then the right approach.

Chrysanthemum carinatum *'Court Jesters'*

Chrysanthemum multicaule *'Moonlight'*

Clarkia *Clarkia*

It seems impossible to write about American plants without the names of Lewis and Clark coming to the surface. It was on their famous expedition in the early years of the nineteenth century that William Clark collected the first seed of the plant that bears his name, Clarkia.

Despite the American origins of clarkias, it's the British who've grown and developed them while few American gardeners seem to grow them. Until the 1920s, new clarkias were being introduced in exquisite individual colors. Then as it became more expensive to maintain a high level of consistency, they faded away and only mixtures were left. Mixtures command a lower price so there's even less incentive for seed companies to keep the quality high – and the downward spiral continues.

Try to avoid those with names such as 'Mixed' or 'Double Mixed' in favor of 'Rhapsody' and 'Love Affair' which are just becoming available and which are blended from seed of distinct colors, each grown and harvested separately.

The colors grown for these formula mixtures are also now listed separately, so we have 'Chieftain', in clear mauve, and the unambiguous 'Apple Blossom' and 'Salmon Queen', the last two first listed in catalogs in the 1920s.

These all make good cut flowers – cut when the first two or three flowers on the spike are open to ensure that the whole spike lasts well. It's well worth sowing a row between the cabbages, and even clumps in a border among shrubs will not miss a few stems cut for a display in the house.

In mixed borders, 'Apple Blossom' looks good with the upright bold spikes of anise hyssop, *Agastache foeniculum* 'Alba', while the stronger-colored 'Salmon Queen' makes a tasteful, if unexpected, neighbor for Oriental poppies in similar shades – just let the clarkias self-sow in autumn; they'll overwinter in many areas and flower with the poppies.

All this so far refers to *Clarkia elegans*, correctly known as *C. unguiculata*; the other long-standing species grown is *Clarkia pulchella*, native to the Pacific Northwest. This is less bold in habit, far more bushy and at 12 in./30 cm. only half the height. The white, 'Snowflake', is the pick and, falling into smaller variegated hostas like 'Ginko Craig' it looks just right. 'Passion for Purple', the other separate color usually available, is a lovely surprise among dark-leaved heucheras such as 'Stormy Seas'.

Clarkia bottae, which has recently migrated from the woodland clearings and chaparral of California to the seed catalogs, is the one species which you see listed under both *Godetia* and

Clarkia bottae 'Amethyst Glow' with the pinks from Limonium sinuatum 'Pastel Shades'.

Clarkia – depending on the catalog. The pretty upward-facing flowers in various shades of bluish-purple come with names like 'Amethyst Glow', 'Lady in Blue', and 'Lilac Blossom'. Their relatively open habit allows them to mingle well with annual phlox and snapdragons, hardy geraniums and low campanulas; we eagerly await a white form.

All these clarkias can be sown direct where they're to flower; if you raise them in containers as half-hardy annuals, grow them cool and make sure that you never let the containers become overcrowded with roots.

RIGHT *The plant of Clarkia pulchella 'Snowflake' at the top, with its divided petals, is the true form of this variety although occasionally plants with broader, undivided petals appear. This reversion often takes place when plants are allowed to self-sow over a number of years without the rogues being removed. In either form, there is a clean purity to the color that really sparkles, as here against the slightly grayish leaves and rose-pink flowers of Geranium* × riversleaianum *'Mavis Simpson'.*

Cleome *Spider Flower*

'What on earth are *they*?' So goes the reaction from the visiting innocent gardener to a bed full of cleomes. Four petals like the ears of a demented pantomime rabbit stand up from the end of each stem in the head of flowers, with the four thread-like stamens hanging below and a rocket-battery of darker buds standing upright in the top of the spike. The effect is unashamedly exotic. Individual plants reach 4 ft./1.2 m. high, or more from an early sowing, and branch impressively if pinched. This exoticism is enhanced by the bold foliage, a valuable feature in itself in early summer. Recent introductions from the wild feature unusually dark foliage but a late flowering season, useless in cooler regions at least. Bringing these characteristics together with existing forms in a simple breeding program could be rewarding.

The names, and the consistency of the coloring in the different varieties, leave something to be desired. As with many open-pollinated varieties that have been around for decades yet are not important economically, the seed producers have been less than thorough in their attention to ensuring that the plants stay true to type. Hence the flowers of 'Violet Queen', never exactly violet in the first place, vary from altogether mauve to opening mauve then aging to blushed white. 'Cherry Queen' is more consistent yet no more cherry than 'Violet Queen' is violet; 'Pink Queen' is, at least, pink while 'Helen Campbell' is certainly the purest white.

The mixture usually entitled 'Color Fountain' is more valuable than many. The flowers are in a sympathetic color range that harmonizes well without culling; plants from the mix are ideal as a feature in themselves planted through an autumn border. Fronted by and mingled among the developing foliage of asters and hardy chrysanthemums, the reckless spider flowers make a splendid precursor to the main business of the border. In a long swaying mass fronted, perhaps, by 'Operetta' China asters in similar shades with their distinctive, quilled balls of spiky color – your jaw will drop. The same idea can be translated to a round bed where cleomes make a relaxed centerpiece that doesn't emphasize the formal shape.

Another, less common, use for cleomes is in containers – but not in the mixed plantings of petunias and lobelia seen alongside porches everywhere; the scale would be farcical. Start them off in early spring, keep moving them into individual pots and pinch them to encourage the characteristic lurching branching, then move them into their final containers in a cold greenhouse before moving them outside. The result will be substantial plants which create a combination of drama and fascination set in a group of three or four outside the front door. Sow in place in May where summers are long and warm; in such zones it self-seeds readily. But beware: do not place them so close to the pathway that they're constantly brushed, for each leaf has a sharp and

LEFT Cleome *'Violet Queen'* may not be especially violet in color but its two-tone flower heads fit well with, at one end of their spectrum, the tall purple flowers of Verbena bonariensis *and, at the other, with white cosmos. Earlier in the season, before the flowers erupt, the dark, bronze-toned foliage of the cleome makes a fascinating contrast with the green leaves of the cosmos.*

RIGHT *Mixtures and single colors can, occasionally, work well together. In front of these ancient espaliered apples, the bold and bright* Nicotiana sylvestris *gives solidity to the mixed plantings, and the cosmos and cleome work especially well together as their color palette is similar, ensuring a natural harmony.*

painful spine at the point where the leaf joins the stem. Cleomes also attract bees – too many, perhaps, for inclusion in children's gardens.

It's also possible to manipulate the height of cleomes a little by starting them later than usual. This not only avoids the requirement for good heat early in the season but allows them to be grown in small gardens at the front of the border. Late sowings will flower on shorter stems, but with little branching and perhaps without the staying power of those sown earlier.

Plant breeders have attempted to create consistently dwarf and naturally branching types but without noticeable success and I suspect that it may never be possible to marigoldize them genetically.

ABOVE *This sumptuous but rather unlikely subtropical-style planting features the yellow-striped leaves of* Canna *'Striata' fronted by the spiky ripples of the blue-gray honey bush,* Melianthus major, *and at the back the bold, dark leaves of* Catalpa x erubescens *'Purpurea', which is cut back each spring to produce the most dramatic leaves. Running through, and somehow not clashing horribly with the cannas, is* Cleome *'Violet Queen'.*

Cobaea Cup-and-Saucer Vine

Vigorous and spectacularly exotic, the Mexican native *Cobaea scandens* is neither a difficult plant nor a rare one. Its seeds are large and easy to sow, it climbs strongly, and a single plant will cover a large area . . . yet relatively few gardeners grow it.

Perhaps its need for a high germination temperature, not less than 70°F/20°C, is a deterrent. But most of us need so few plants that four seeds split between two 3½ in./9 cm. pots on a windowsill is plenty. Sow each large flat seed, on edge, just under the surface of the potting mix and cover it with plastic wrap. Germination can be irregular, but remove the plastic when the first seedling is through or, better still, peel it back halfway. Leave the seedlings to develop at their own pace then pot each up individually in 3½ in./9 cm. pots, moving them later into 5 in./12.5 cm. pots. Keep them growing on at 60–65°F/12–15°C, then harden them off carefully before planting out after the last frost.

Cobaea scandens needs support. The desperate tendrils at the end of every divided leaf ceaselessly search for it. They need support in their pots, where they can be tied to a single cane in their early stages, then pinched soon after their move into large pots, and trained up three more canes spaced evenly around the edge. They can, there is no doubt, be difficult to manage in their early weeks and are apt to strangle their neighbors on the greenhouse bench.

In the garden, trellising is the most effective support system: wire or especially plastic netting can sag under the weight of what, in warm areas, may be a large volume of growth unless it's fixed securely to a wall at regular intervals. On a sunny wall, and with good support, growth of 15–25 ft./4.5–7.5 m.

Cobaea scandens

in one summer is possible, so guiding the growth through a shrub is usually impractical. In mild climates cup-and-saucer vine is a good perennial, overwintering happily and flowering from May to October; sow direct in zones 9 and warmer.

Cobaea looks impressive given a large space on a wall of its own, but in cooler areas may only thrive with the extra coziness that a sunny wall provides. In warmer areas it will even make a wild and rambling hedge of growth on a wire fence . . . the warmer the summers, the more situations it will relish.

A problem can occur when cobaea is grown on a wall – the lower growth may not be well covered by foliage and flowers. The trick is to plant another, less vigorous climber to cling to the lower reaches of the cobaea. Canary vine, *Tropaeolum peregrinum*, is a good choice; it covers well and looks ravishing as it mingles into the purple flowers of the cobaea. A bushier alternative is *Mina lobata*. This unlikely relative of the convolvulus appreciates the same warm conditions as the cobaea and its shrubbier growth brings the whole planting forward into the border a little so it integrates better with its neighbors. Its flowers start in warm red, then mature through orange, yellow, and finally white. Can you imagine it with the deep purple cobaea bells?

There's also a less common white form of *C. scandens*, 'Alba', (the two forms look good mingled together) and this is better underplanted with the lemon and white bicolored *Mina lobata* 'Citronella' to make an altogether cooler, sharper sun-loving association. Many years ago there was a variegated form, rare then and unheard of now.

Convolvulus Dwarf Morning Glory

For many gardeners, the association between these hardy annual convolvulus and the dreaded bindweed with its racing roots is simply too much – banishment from the garden is total and rarely reconsidered unless the enlightenment of experience overcomes prejudice. But just look at what they're missing!

In cooler climates in particular, the flared convolvulus trumpets (for once the word 'trumpet' really does describe the shape of the flowers) are a real treat. The blue is of a depth and richness unknown in any other annuals, in almost any other flowers of a comparative size. When gardeners see convolvulus at their best they almost always seem surprised and delighted, yet as soon as they hear the botanical name, their enthusiasm wanes.

Annual convolvulus fall into two groups: bushy types based on *Convolvulus tricolor*, which are covered here, and climbers based on what used to be called *Convolvulus major* but which is now more correctly known as *Ipomoea purpurea*, the common morning glory – these are found under *Ipomoea* (pages 102–103).

The star of them all is 'Royal Ensign', sometimes called 'Blue Ensign'. With flowers like a petunia, only a little smaller, the throat is like the chuckling sun on the Teletubbies – but a great deal less irritating. A slightly ragged white star then splays into the rich blue outer edging.

In a border which is focused tightly on blue flowers, with *Lobelia* 'Blue Wings', *Salvia farinacea* 'Victoria', *Phlox* 'Blue Beauty', and the sometimes hard-to-find *Salpiglossis* 'Kew Blue', the bright spark from those yellow throats just makes the blues seem even more intensely blue.

Red, rose, and white are also available separately (all have that same yellow throat and white star) and mixtures occasionally feature a very pretty palest sky-blue form which I've not yet seen listed separately.

The white, with its creamy throat, is ideal as a petunia substitute, and shines like satin, even on dull days. The red can be a little variable but at its best has a hazy maroon tinge; the rose is perhaps the least successful as the color can be murky. The mixture may be listed as 'Ensign Mixed' or 'Flagship'.

The Ensign Series is just the right size. Bushy enough for the front of the border, or even as a low cover in the middle ground, it's also lax enough for baskets and other containers, where the coloring and habit of 'Royal Ensign' can be invaluable. 'Royal Ensign' is pushy enough to insinuate itself among other plants yet not so dominant that it smothers them. 'Blue Flash', and the 'Dwarf Rainbow Flash' mixture are less than half the height and so less adaptable.

It would be a mistake to stretch the comparison with petunias too far, but convolvulus do have the advantage of larger, more manageable seed and seedlings which are also robust enough to handle easily. They germinate well at much lower temperatures than petunias, but, unfortunately, they still lack the color range and perform better in hot, dry summers.

Convolvulus tricolor *'Royal Ensign'*

RIGHT *Even the pugnacious habit of* Salvia viridis *'Claryssa White' and 'Claryssa Pink' allows the persistent trails of* Convolvulus *'Royal Ensign' to peep through. Although both salvia and convolvulus are tough enough to be sown in the open ground in many areas, if you're planning a border, careful sowing in a cool greenhouse and pricking out into individual pots ensures more precise planting.*

Coreopsis Calliopsis and Coreopsis

The catalogs do us a disservice. In some, the *only* coreopsis in the list is 'Early Sunrise'; but, while this is useful as a perennial that flowers prolifically in its first summer, to list only this is to ignore the invaluable, truly annual sorts. This will not happen here.

The 'coreopsis' group is something of a botanical bombsite, filled with the debris resulting from the demolition of *Leptosyne*, *Bidens*, *Calliopsis*, *Cosmidium*, as well as *Coreopsis*. The convenient convention of listing the true annuals under *Calliopsis* and the perennials under *Coreopsis* seems to have been abandoned. Varieties of the native American wildflower, *Coreopsis tinctoria*, sometimes listed under *Calliopsis bicolor*, are highly prolific, sparsely bushy annuals in yellow, chestnut, and almost scarlet. These sparky, long-season daisies are invaluable companions to marigolds; in the same general color range, their lighter air and slender foliage create a quiet contrast.

There are two main groups. The taller reach about 2–3 ft./60–90 cm. in height and are represented by 'T&M Originals' – hardly variable enough to be called a mixture, flowers differ largely in the size of the mahogany center on the deep yellow petals. The closely related Texas native *Cosmidium* (correctly *Thelesperma*) 'Brunette' is similar, but more uniform. Both are superb mixed border annuals, although requiring twiggy brushwood support against rainstorms. Both are delightful among yellow crocosmias, and with goldenrods or in front of dark-leaved cotinus; both make good cut flowers for informal bouquets. Sow forms of *C. tinctoria* direct as they don't transplant well.

Coreopsis *'Mahogany Midget'*

Most coreopsis are shorter, ranging in height from 10–12 in./20–30 cm. 'Mahogany Midget' has none of the ugly squatness of some dwarf annuals, while 'Baby Gold' is self-descriptive; 'Dwarf Mixed' is usually a blend of the two. 'Mahogany Midget' is excellent with *Linaria* 'Fantasia Yellow'.

More rarely seen, but first introduced from Arkansas in 1823, 'Tiger Stripes' is a mix derived from *C. radiata*, with slender petals in various patterns of orange, mahogany, and yellow. Invaluable in "marigoldments" – blends of flowers in the chestnut, mahogany, rust, lemon, yellow, orange, and gold shades of marigolds – its slim petals are a refreshing contrast to double French marigolds. 'Mardi Gras' is a modern dwarf equivalent.

But I glossed over 'Early Sunrise' . . . . This variety, and the similar 'Sunray', can also be treated as biennials. Sown in summer and planted in autumn, they will make larger plants and flower more prolifically.

Finally, there's one species, which, as I write, is not listed in catalogs but which I mention by way of encouragement to order them, should they it surface. *C. maritima* is a bright, noticeably succulent plant which develops enormous tubers where it grows as a sprawling perennial on its native Californian shoreline. In gardens, it's a bright annual for sowing direct and reaches about 18 in./45 cm. in height.

Coreopsis douglasii is shorter, its deeply-cut dark green foliage being rather bushy, and its slender-stemmed, bright yellow daisies standing up well; the whole plant reaches about 12 in./30 cm.

Cosmos Cosmos

Cosmos. . . a name hinting at star quality – and quite rightly, too. These plants are currently undergoing a powerful revival; in recent years plant breeders have been turning their attention to these relations of the more flamboyant dahlias, with noticeable success. Two things have been on their minds: reviving some of the wonderful lost colors and flower forms from the past, and making advances which enable the use of cosmos in more ways. And this is one of those cases where the introduction of new, more dwarf varieties has been no bad thing.

The two main groups of cosmos are noticeably different and both have seen improvements or revivals. The Mexican native, *Cosmos bipinnatus,* is naturally a tall plant, reaching about 4 ft./ 1.2 m., with large but simple daisy-like flowers. In most forms its fresh green, finely cut foliage is valuable from soon after planting time, although some seed stocks develop sparse leafage which reveals too much stem and provides a poor background for the flowers.

Tall, single-flowered forms in reds, pinks and white have been available for many years and have been grown commercially for cutting. Developments for this market have led to the revival of semi-double types such as 'Psyche', with fluffy groups of shorter petals in the center of the flower, and the unique 'Sea Shells', with each petal rolled into a tube. In single colors we now have dark-eyed types like 'Daydream', and pale flowers with magenta lacing like the rather variable 'Picotee', and 'Pied Piper Red'.

All these have proved invaluable plants in mixed borders, their loose open habit being much more companionable with perennials and shrubs than chunkier annuals. And enough single colors are available to make carefully planned color schemes possible; 'Purity' in clean white is an especially valuable form.

With 'Sonata', the height was reduced to around 2 ft./60 cm. The first plants of the award-winning 'Sonata White' were unusual in being strangely flat-topped with most of the flowers set in a single plane above the foliage. More recently, plants of 'Sonata' have grown a little larger and developed a slightly looser, more rounded habit – an improvement to be sure, but perhaps the result of the seed growers being less than rigorous in keeping it to its original specification.

'Sonata White' is a wow planted with bronze-leaved forms of *Pennisetum alopecuroides,* as is 'Sonata Carmine'. In the larger sorts, matching 'Purity' with *Buddleja davidii* 'White Profusion'

Cosmos *'Pied Piper Red'*

OVERLEAF The reduced height of Cosmos *'Sonata White' allows it to mingle intimately with other plants in this small garden setting. Here, it's settled in alongside the slender vertical spikes of* Salvia farinacea *'White Victory' and* Nicotiana *'Lime Green'.*

If you find that the 'Sonata' cosmos is only available as a mixture, as is so often the case, then move the plants on into 5 in./12.5 cm. pots and the first flowers will be open at planting time. You can then separate the whites from the pink and carmine shades which can be planted in situations that better suit their color. Notice how the finely dissected cosmos foliage makes a fine background for the broader leaves of the zinnia seedling.

or 'Picotee' with a dark-leaved cotinus guarantees a sharp intake of breath. 'Dazzler', in its rich velvety crimson, stands out boldly in front of a silver-leaved shrub like *Elaeagnus* 'Quicksilver'; in front of native ninebark, *Physocarpus opulifolius* 'Diablo', it blends to make a richly sumptuous planting. Perillas and heucheras in the foreground, could complete the picture.

Well-established plants provide the best show. It's advisable to start the seeds no later than mid-spring and move the plants on into 5 in./12.5 cm. pots for planting out. The first flowers are often opening at this stage so rogues can be segregated and individual plants selected from mixtures. In many areas, you can also sow seed outside, where it's to flower, in late spring.

Although *Cosmos bipinnatus* and its forms are true annuals, they can be rooted from cuttings, a process probably of little interest to gardeners but which helps plant breeders enormously. The other group, based on *C. sulphureus*, are true perennials and are more closely related to both the chocolate-colored and chocolate-scented *C. atrosanguineus* and to dahlias.

The tallest of these is about the height of the shortest of the *C. bipinnatus* types, around 2 ft./60 cm. All prefer warm summer conditions and are rarely successful in cooler zones except in containers and cozy conditions in rich soil. The color range is limited to reds, oranges, and yellows, but most are semi-double and more dependably so than forms of *C. bipinnatus*.

Raising forms of *C. sulphureus* by sowing outside is much less successful, partly because seed is more expensive and packets usually contain far fewer seeds. And in cooler areas especially, growth of *C. sulphureus* may not be sufficiently rapid for good flowering-sized plants to develop from a late-spring sowing.

The Ladybird Series, reaching up to 12 in./30 cm., and the more vigorous Sunny Series, growing to twice that size or more, come in just red, orange, and yellow. There may be a little variation in the shades of each color and in the degree of doubling but not sufficiently to prove uncomfortable to the gardener. They're all great sun lovers, with the shades harmonizing well; all sparkle with *Helichrysum petiolare* 'Limelight' arching through.

LEFT At Wave Hill in the Bronx, New York, this dramatic variegated Canna 'Striata' is fronted by the dense feathery domes of Bassia (formerly Kochia) scoparia – the burning bush, well known for transforming itself into a rich mound of fire in autumn. Sprawling through is 'Sunny Orange-Red', a semi-double form of Cosmos sulphureus which needs the hot New York summers to give its best.

RIGHT The feathery foams of the cosmos foliage threaten to overwhelm the 'Nero di Toscana' kale but this is a tough plant which can hold its own against most competition. 'Pied Piper Red' is the first of a new series of seashell-style cosmos in single colors. Alongside is one of the old, rediscovered Victorian striped French marigolds adding to the freshness with green leaves as well as the two-tone flowers.

Delphinium Larkspur

Two, indeed three, very different plants fit here – and only one is a true annual. It is possible to grow the herbaceous border delphiniums, hybrids of *Delphinium elatum*, as annuals; sow very early, grow on strongly, and plant out in early summer. For the back of an annual border, the Southern Series has proved outstanding – as long as their early season absence is tolerable. The slim spikes, considered old-fashioned by delph buffs (but that's beside the point), actually fit in better with annuals than the fatter spikes of the slightly earlier-flowering, but altogether less dependable, Pacific Giants.

But it's the truly annual larkspurs, now correctly classified as *Consolida*, which have been such a revelation to me in recent years. It's the less familiar of the group which have proved so valuable, but let's dispose of the more traditional types first.

The densely packed spikes of 'Hyacinth Flowered' and the Imperial Series often have a crude, unfriendly habit – a long way from *Consolida ambigua* from which they were developed. Stiff and upright in growth, nevertheless the taller mixtures and some of the delightful single colors are invaluable as cut flowers. They're also very attractive when dried. The exquisite blue-and-white bicolored 'Frosted Skies' and the intriguing 'Earl Grey' in dusky pink are the pick; grow them in rows where they'll brighten the rhubarb. In the border, however, they sit uneasily, unless acting for perennials in a very traditional herbaceous planting.

But there's a less well-known, less developed group, closer to the *Consolida regalis* from which they're derived, that has an airy and relaxed demeanor; these are indispensable. The two featured most often in catalogs are 'Blue Cloud' and 'Snow Cloud'. The flowers are single, five-petalled and, massed on a well developed plant, they truly have the look of a cloud of inky or milky butterflies, fluttering prettily on the breeze. The plants branch repeatedly, the flowers keep coming, the growth is never so dense as to crowd out neighbors. Although the 2½ ft./45 cm. plants are not thoroughly self-supporting, neither are they so dense as to smother their neighbors if they flop. In fact, the most delightful and surprising associations can come about when snapdragons, verbenas, dianthus, godetia, painted tongue, and other determined annuals find their way through the clouds of color. And as the larkspurs lean, new flowering shoots emerge from the leaf joints along the stem to add to the intimate confusion.

Although happy sown direct, it is best to raise these varieties in cool conditions indoors and plant them out from 3 in./7 cm. pots in thoughtfully planned positions to create the most effective intermingled plantings. Interplant them among and alongside other annuals rather than in a fat block, remembering that they may reach over 2 ft./60 cm. in height and spread.

Consolida ambigua

With 'Sonnet Rose' snapdragons, the quivering billows of *Consolida* 'Snow Cloud' are like foam from the ocean around besuited bathers languidly rolling in the surf. The more upright cuttings-raised verbenas like the mauve 'Lila' or 'Pastel Pink', rather than the flatter growing Temari and Tapien series, also make good companions.

Delphinium grandiflorum is the other species grown, a perennial though one which requires good drainage to ensure its winter survival. 'Blue Butterfly' is a gorgeous royal blue, 'Sky Blue' is self-descriptive. Both will sulk and may fade away if overwatered in their pots.

RIGHT *In this bold grouping, the powerful magenta of crown-pink,* Lychnis coronaria, *and* Consolida *'Blue Cloud' larkspur make a startling and unlikely association. While the magenta and blue create a contrast, a more robust white larkspur among the silver lychnis leaves helps it all come together*

RIGHT *The stray white wands of* Consolida *'Snow Cloud' fall into the foreground while green-edged midnight foliage of* Solenostemon (Coleus) *'Black Heart' fills the background. It sets off that most valuable, yet underused, gray foliage plant* Plecostachys serpyllifolia, *often incorrectly labelled as a micro form of* Helichrysum petiolare.

RIGHT Trachelium 'Passion in Violet' was bred as a bushy pot plant but it makes a valuable outdoor annual from an early sowing; its mauve, but perhaps not violet, umbels throwing repeatedly, and ever taller, all summer. Here, Consolida 'Blue Cloud', with the matching blue cape forget-me-not, Anchusa capensis 'Blue Bird' (at 18 in./45 cm. twice the height of 'Blue Angel' and so more useful), strikes boldly through the center to open its vibrant flowers.

BELOW The Exquisite Series of larkspurs is intended for use as cut flowers and can develop rather overcrowded spikes for an informal planting. Here, once the spike of 'Exquisite Salmon Beauty' has begun to lean under the pressure from neighbors (in this case the autumnal foliage of Lysimachia ciliata 'Firecracker'), small side shoots emerge which are less crowded, more delicate and which peep through the foliage creating interesting associations.

Dianthus Pinks and Sweet William

Garden pinks are among the best-loved of perennial flowers for their old-fashioned charm, their scent and their long flowering season, so why are the annual pinks and their various relatives not equally popular? It's true that some, like 'Raspberry Parfait', combine a squat habit with garish and smudgy coloring in a way which endears them to few; many even lack scent as a redeeming feature. Chiefly, though, gardeners are disappointed to find that these are not annual versions of perennial pinks; this frustration prevents recognition of the value of the wide range of forms and colors in annual dianthus.

The annual pinks developed from *Dianthus chinensis*, *D. superbus*, and some with genes from the sweet William, *D. barbatus*, are all single flowered and closer in style to a traditional bedding plant than a border pink. They make well-branched, twiggy little plants with flowers concentrated towards the top. They flower early and long but may rest in the heat of the summer when they can be snipped back and soaked to promote new flowers.

The Telstar, Princess, and the thirteen color Ideal Series are the most widely available and some individual colors are superb – although mixtures are more frequently seen in catalogs. There are many combinations you could try. 'Telstar Crimson', with deep red flowers and dark foliage to match, is good in front of *Cosmos atrosanguineus* or *Dahlia* 'Bednall Beauty'. 'Ideal Deep Violet' is uniquely rich in color with a pale edge to its petals and is warm and sultry with *Solenostemon* (*Coleus*) 'Rob Roy'. 'Telstar Picotee' (red with a white edge) is the choice when you need a bicolor with a little more style than

those in the Parfait Series – try it alongside 'Venus' geranium. 'Princess White' is a clear, pure shade effortlessly impressive with 'Sonnet Rose' snapdragons or *Laurentia* 'Blue Stars'. 'Telstar Color Magician' is unique with flowers which open pink and fade to white – a plant association in a single plant.

The Feather Series, in red and in white (sometimes listed as 'Crimsonia' and 'Snowdonia'), is rather different and, sadly, very hard to find. They have a loose, open, airy habit, with large deeply fringed flowers and, if planted in boxes or baskets, they trail enticingly and blend well with trailing lobelia and even with petunias. In beds and borders their habit and persistence allow them to mingle intimately with other plants to create striking and endearing associations.

Seed-raised carnations have developed in two absolutely opposite directions. The taller Chabaud types, carrying names such as 'Chabaud Giant Double Mixed', 'Luminette' and especially 'Champion', make superb cut flowers, blooming prolifically in their first year from seed. The color range is unexpectedly broad and includes pretty picotees as well as pure colors, including yellow. All are well scented (some intoxicatingly so). While a mixed planting may look a little too jazzy in a herbaceous border, single colors are occasionally available, and the mixtures are unrivalled in rows in the vegetable or cutting garden.

At the same time, carnations have also been developed as pot plants: the Knight, Lillipot, and Monarch series stand out. In sheltered places, these also make good plants for containers and in warm gardens thrive in the open ground. The Monarch Series, in seven colors, is the pick

Dianthus barbatus *cultivar*

Dianthus *'White Feather'*

RIGHT *The unique suitability of the Feather dianthus for informal plant groupings is shown in this intermingled summer planting. The slender upright flowering shoots of 'Red Feather' rise from its spreading stems through the dark foliage of purple-leaved basil and 'Breakaway Red' geraniums. Behind is Amaranthus 'Hopi Red Dye' with the cuttings-raised Verbena 'Temari Red' behaving the same way.*

with strong scent and good performance in containers; there they need neat companions like the smaller coleus, 'Inky Fingers' for example, or silver *Senecio cineraria* 'Silver Dust', to prevent their being smothered.

Sweet William, *D. barbatus*, can be difficult to use in the garden. The problem is that apart from a few justifiably difficult-to-find varieties such as 'Roundabout' which have been turned into dwarf annuals, these are uncomfortably late-flowering biennials. This means they're often still at their best when summer annuals are waiting to be planted and there's an understandable reluctance to tear them out.

The answer is to grow them not in exclusively temporary spring plantings, but in spaces in perennial and mixed borders. However, then the problem is that the captivating single colors, with their old fashioned picotee and bicolored flower forms, are so hard to find. You may only find the admittedly irresistible 'Sooty', in the deepest blood-red with a ring of white specks in the center and foliage which deepens to crimson as the plant develops. This is a wonderful plant, seen at its best towards the front of the border, surrounded by fresh green foliage where its deep coloring can be appreciated.

LEFT *White foxgloves are superlative biennials for shady glades. Here, with grasses, columbines, and Dicentra* spectabilis, *they stand pure and upright gleaming in the green glade. They will self-sow freely, often flowering most impressively in their first year then tailing off noticeably.*

Digitalis Foxglove

The foxglove of the English woods and Scottish hills has long been cultivated in gardens. American settlers were inspired to bring plants to the new country, where foxgloves quickly became both naturalized and cherished in gardens. Both here and in their native land, selection, change, and development were inevitable, as individual plants appreciated for their special beauty were preferred over the more commonplace.

In some wild populations, up to a third of all foxglove plants may be white, but otherwise they vary relatively little. Whites may be spotted or unspotted, although those without bold markings often feature a tawny ghosting where the spots might have been. Ugly forms known as 'Monstrosa' or 'Peloric Form', in which the topmost flower is opened from its familiar tubular shape to a large flat saucer, have been known for centuries and are still occasionally seen in the wild. Interesting curiosities, they have little else to recommend them. Foxgloves have developed more impressively in terms of stature, color, spotting, and the arrangement of the flower spike; these features can be related to the way in which plants are used in the garden.

In their natural forms and colors, sweeps or scatterings of foxgloves are at home in shady naturalistic plantings with their European native companions like male fern (*Dryopteris filix-mas*), weeping wood sedge (*Carex pendula*), and nettle-leaved bellflower (*Campanula trachelium*). White foxgloves are perfect plants for woodland planting. But their bold rosettes, while attractive in themselves, are pugnacious and pushy, shouldering out more delicate neighbors.

Choose carefully which plants to retain; the rest can go for compost.

Foxgloves will usually self-sow with all too much enthusiasm so it's important to deadhead the spikes as they fade. Watch them carefully, for the lowest seed pods will be ripe and dropping their seed while the upper flowers are still at their best; it may be necessary to sacrifice a few days' flowers to prevent the appearance of sheets of self-sown seedlings, most of which must be removed. Leave just a few exactly where they will best show themselves.

In such naturalistic situations, the more highly developed forms look out of place. New colors, including yellow and the gorgeous 'Apricot', have come from centuries of selection and breeding; in 'Giant Spotted' and 'Glittering Prizes' spots have merged into bold blotches, while 'Excelsior' carries its flowers all round the spike rather than elegantly on one side as in the wild forms. These forms may be unsuitable when used in wild gardens, but look like improvements on the wild species if you use them in colorful and sophisticated borders.

There are practical difficulties associated with using foxgloves in borders. Although all these forms of *Digitalis purpurea* often behave as short-lived perennials, their first flowering season is their most spectacular, and the larger the plants the greater the spectacle. Traditionally, you sow seed outside in midsummer, thin and then transplant seedlings into their flowering sites in early fall, by which time they've reached quite a substantial size.

Digitalis purpurea *f.* albiflora *(two forms)*

Digitalis *'Giant Spotted'*

But few modern gardens have room to raise such large plants, and in today's crowded borders, with so many more autumn flowers now used, there's little space to set the plants, and the later they go out the less impressive the show. Additionally, in poor garden soil much of that soil may be lost from the roots in the transplanting process, thus retarding development and reducing the spectacle.

Raising them in pots can solve the problem. Sow in late spring then move the plants into 3½ in./9 cm., 5 in./12.5 cm. and then 8 in./20 cm. pots as they grow; the result will be large and luxuriant plants – and you will probably need fewer than you expect; they can be set out 2 ft./60 cm. apart. Because they have such a tight and undisturbed rootball they can be planted later, when there is more room in the autumn border, and still make a staggering succession of spikes from the leaf joints in the rosette. Any leftovers can be simply moved into containers to make impressive doorway displays.

Like hollyhocks and sweet Williams, foxgloves have also been turned from biennials into annuals – to no one's great advantage. 'Foxy' is reckoned not only to be substantially shorter than the 4 ft./1.2 m. plus of most varieties, but is supposed to flower in its first summer from an early spring sowing. When it was first introduced this was actually true – its choice as an All-America Selection seemed to reward its uniform dwarfness. Its deterioration is revealed most clearly in its height: when I first saw it the plants looked very fine, if a little odd, at just over 2 ft./60 cm.; more recently 4 ft./1.2 m. has been seen; treated as a biennial they almost match the towering 'Excelsior'.

LEFT *The slim and startlingly upright spikes of* Digitalis parviflora *stand erect among the more languid growth and big pale bells of* Campanula takesimana. *Like most species, this foxglove is actually a short-lived perennial which produces a good plant when sown in summer as a biennial and will then self-sow in any reasonably sunny well-drained soil. It seems as happy there as in damper conditions in partial shade.*

RIGHT *The crushed raspberry and cream color of* Digitalis × mertonensis, *a hybrid between* D. purpurea *and* D. grandiflora, *demands a careful choice of companions and, in this town garden, white works unexpectedly well. The pure white form of* Campanula persicifolia *is as likely to self-seed as the foxglove. The back of the garden gleams brightly with white* D. purpurea.

Eccremocarpus *Glory Flower*

Forsythias make a bright and buttery splash in early spring but goodness, aren't they dull in summer? Viburnums, weigela, flowering currants . . . none have anything to offer for many crucial months. Well, here's the answer: all are perfect hosts for climbers and in particular for eccremocarpus.

The Chilean glory flower, *Eccremocarpus scaber*, makes a great deal of bushy growth and because of this it needs stout support. The tendrils cling securely but it pays to plant on the shady side of the shrub so that the shoots snake their way through to emerge into the sun; in this way the whole shrub supports the climber. (If you plant on the sunny side, the shoots lurch away from where support is provided since growth tends towards the best light.)

In cool areas planting on a sunny fence or wall is preferable. Eccremocarpus will cling well to trellis or wire mesh fixed to the wall, or a wall-grown evergreen *Ceanothus americanus* makes a good host. In such situations this naturally woody climber may well survive the winter in gardens where otherwise it might be killed. When it does survive, only a brutal spring pruning of old woody growth will ensure another prolific summer-long display.

The fat inflated pods burst with flat, shiny black seeds and seedlings may spring up, especially in gravel and often some distance from the parent plant. The soil under wall-grown specimens can be dense with bright, fresh seedlings in late spring. These seedlings are vigorous enough to flower in their first summer in all but the coldest gardens and flowers may unexpectedly appear from the foliage of shrubs acting as surprise hosts.

Mixtures are most often found in catalogs. They have names such as 'Tresco Hybrids', 'Fireworks', and 'Carnival Time', but they pose a problem to the thoughtful plant arranger: young plants are rarely in flower at planting time so there's little opportunity to select separate colors from the mixtures for special positions. If only mixtures are available, the only approach is to plant individual plants in their own positions, cross your fingers and hope for the best!

The wild species, in orange, is also often listed and this sits best against plain green foliage, although I've also seen it growing up into flannel bush, *Fremontodendron* 'California Glory' – a startling combination; the yellow goes well with *Ceanothus* 'Puget Blue'; 'Tresco Cream', in almost white with a hint of yellowish orange, would make a fitting partner for cup-and-saucer vine, *Cobaea scandens* 'Alba'.

The pink, and the dusky red of 'Tresco Crimson', are better seen in close-up on a pillar or the side of a sunny doorway as their colors have little penetration and make less impact from the back of a border.

Eccremocarpus scaber

Eryngium Miss Willmott's Ghost

The most important single element in successful gardening is learning to see. Being open to seeing and understanding the landscape of the garden and how it affects you physically and emotionally is crucial – as is being sharp to the garden's details, the plants.

Eryngium giganteum is a biennial familiar to many U.K. gardeners but is sadly absent in many U.S. gardens. It is often wrongly thought to be a thistle by the less observant – the flower head, the flowers and the seeds are all entirely different in structure. So, by association, it's often burdened with the reputations of unrelated plants like the bold, statuesque but unstable thistle, *Onopordum nervosum*, and the entertainingly named *Silybum marianum*, with its pretty silver-veined foliage, overwhelming growth, and its invasive self-seeding. (It's still well worth growing, if only for the fun of imparting its generic name, pronounced "Silly bum," to more straight-laced garden visitors). *Eryngium giganteum* is better behaved than either. It's known as Miss Willmott's Ghost because seed surreptitiously scattered by the great, turn-of-the-century English gardener bloomed ghostly-silver, marking her passing, months after she had visited a garden. Many gardeners grow it and it's always the same; or at least it was . . . .

Botanist Martyn Rix has a good eye. On a trip to Trabzon in Turkey he saw a variety of *E. giganteum* which was different from the familiar form. He collected seed and introduced

it to British gardens. Now known as 'Silver Ghost', the silvery bracts which make up so much of the flower's attractiveness are larger than in the usual form and their dissections are different; the flowers also last longer and are carried in larger heads. Tramping about in the wilds of Turkey few of us would have spotted this distinction. But this is just one of many cases where opportunism and "being open to seeing" has led to the introduction of a good new plant.

This species is a genuine biennial. If you have enough seed, simply copy Miss Willmott and fling a handful through any border which would benefit from silvery exclamations. The seedlings make an impact from an early age with their broad, stiff silver leaves, glinting in the sunlight – so ensure that they're not overwhelmed by their neighbors. Otherwise, sow in pots in early summer, move the seedlings into 3½ in./ 9 cm. pots, then plant in sun or partial shade in carefully chosen sites before the roots become too congested. In the years that follow, the seed sowing will take care of itself.

LEFT *The flower heads in the dramatic branching structure of* Eryngium giganteum *open successively over a long period and here are offset very effectively against* Heuchera 'Palace Purple', *itself an excellent spring bedder when raised from a good stock of seed. The questing stems of* Geranium x riversleaianum 'Mavis Simpson' *clamber in from below.*

Erysimum *Wallflower*

Wallflowers (formerly *Cheiranthus*) are a peculiarly British phenomenon. Originally native to seaside cliffs, they're still largely a staple of British gardens where their relaxing colors and sharp scent are an integral feature of both traditional and more modern displays. In the U.S., however, they are greatly overlooked.

These spring-flowering, sun-loving biennials have two great attractions. Their color, to start. Few plants cover their range, from deepest blood-reds and purples, to golds through primrose, peach, and other pastel shades to almost white. Their enjoyably ragged spikes of slightly floppy-petaled flowers are not only colorful but unexpectedly endearing (like the cheerful urchins, extras in a PBS Dickens dramatization). And then there's that scent – nothing can compare with the fragrance of just a few wallflowers after a spring shower.

The trick is that they prefer cool summers with nights below 70°F/21C. In truth, wallflowers are dwarf, drought-tolerant shrubs; some varieties are even raised from cuttings for planting in informal Mediterranean-style gardens and sunny borders. More traditionally, wallflowers flower prolifically the following spring from seed sown in summer. The seedlings are thinned then transplanted into nursery rows outside; in autumn the plants are dug up and moved to their flowering sites. They can be very leafy at this stage and, as this is combined with a tendency for the soil to drop off their sparse roots in the moving process, it's easy to understand why sometimes they fail to settle.

Amazingly, wallflowers are still sold in Britain in bundles of a dozen or twenty plants, almost invariably in mixed colors only and with all the soil shaken from the roots. They're pulled from a bucket of murky water and wrapped in old newspaper – the better to soak your car seat on the way home. Wallflowers deserve better; in particular, retaining soil on the roots is crucial (and is this not a basic prerequisite with all plants?). In the U.S., plants are often sold so small they never achieve their natural boldness. Do not buy these. Buy them grown in large pots, or, better still, raise your own.

Wallflowers germinate well in cool conditions and you can sow them in a cold frame, or even in pots outside in cool summers, then prick them out directly into 3 in./7.5 cm. pots. From here they can go in nursery rows in the traditional manner and from there to their final homes. Alternatively, you can move them into 5 in./12.5 cm. pots, although watering more than a few may prove exasperating. Wallflowers benefit from spending at least part of their lives in pots. When finally planted in fall their rootballs hold together far better than those of plants raised in the traditional way.

There are three groups of varieties. The five-color Prince Series,

Erysimum 'Ellen Willmott'

RIGHT *Traditionally, wallflowers are used in bedding schemes but here again they work well in a mixed planting. Under shrubs and among perennials, 'Purple Queen' wallflowers blend with 'Recreado' tulips to create a dark but hardly somber association. The remains of the tulip foliage will disappear among the spreading perennials and the tulips can be left in place, as the shrub roots dry the soil out sufficiently in high summer to suit the tulips.*

from Japan, is the smallest. These are best suited to raising in pots and also to planting in containers, especially with dwarf tulips, hybrids of *T. greigii* and *T. kauffmanniana*. The habit of the Prince Series can be rather flat-topped and in the open ground plants may perform poorly; when other, softer colors become available it will be more tempting to overlook its shortcomings. Where a short variety is needed in the open, the four-color Bedder Series is more dependable.

However, it's among the tallest types that the best colors – twelve altogether – are found. The sultry 'Blood Red' makes a bold contrast with 'White Triumphator' tulips or in a closer color companionship with *Tulipa* 'Queen of Night'. The rich-colored wallflower 'Purple Queen' ('Ruby Gem' is always given as a synonym but it is, actually, purple) is a wonderful shade while the least common is also one of the prettiest: *Erysimum* 'Ellen Willmott' is rarely listed but its pale peachy tones are both unexpected and gorgeous. I like it on its own, in a small bed, perhaps by the front door, where its color can be admired and its fragrance savored. Taller tulips are also most effective; they have a natural looseness of habit which allows them to blend well. 'Cloth of Gold' wallflowers, for example, look good with cream and green 'Spring Green' tulips and with blue sparks from one of the taller forget-me-nots planted out at the same time. A similar effect in a mixed border comes from planting the wallflowers around the perennial *Brunnera macrophylla*.

LEFT *This spring planting in a small suburban garden shows how wallflowers can be integrated into naturalistic designs without looking out of place. The whole arrangement is yellow and deep purple. Lysimachia ciliata 'Firecracker' with its deepest purple, almost black leaves (there are yellow flowers in summer) and 'Ravenswing', the dark-leaved form of the British native* Anthriscus sylvestris, *set the dark tones. Narcissus 'Petrel', with its many-flowered heads of creamy flowers, and the flowers of the anthriscus sit at the other end of the spectrum with the pale yellow of 'Primrose Monarch' wallflowers and the yellow leaves of feverfew adding sparks. 'Mellow Yellow' columbines, with yellow leaves and white flowers, neatly take in both of the paler colors.*

Eschscholzia *California Poppy*

One of the great joys of writing this book has been that again and again I find I can say that the plants are easy to grow – and so it is here. Too often, enthusiasm for growing a plant so extravagantly praised by an author and covetously desired by the reader is dampened by the long and detailed description of its very particular cultural requirements which follows. Not so here. (Well, I should amend that to say they may pout in very hot weather, but other than that . . . .)

To begin: even the most mean-spirited seed companies provide a generous fill of seeds in packets of California poppies – two or three hundred is common. Germination of California poppy seeds is trouble-free and speedy, given at least some sunshine, from a direct sowing at any time from spring to midsummer. Flowering continues for weeks, even months, and their own self-sown seedlings may start to flower at just the time the parent plant starts to run out of ooomph. In mild areas they can be sown in the autumn.

So, they grow like weeds . . . surely there's more to it than that? Of course. California poppies are simply the most exquisite of all the genuine annuals. Whether setting the whole landscape afire in their native habitat or as a single plant growing by a gravel driveway, their simplicity is captivating. The harmonious variations in the rippling of their petals, the delicate intermingling of shades, their flower colors – sparky or soft and now including more pretty pastels – the fine foliage, with grays becoming more widespread than the usual green. And the altogether happy conjunction of flower and foliage is delightful, the broad petals contrasting with finely dissected leaves.

The state flower of California,

Eschscholzia californica, is generally yellow, sometimes with a few orange spots at the base of the petals, although more than ninety wild forms have been described by botanists. Breeding has widened the color range impressively, shortened the height, added doubling and fluting to the petals and silver shades to the foliage; 'Rose Chiffon' is recognizably an eschscholzia but clearly different from the wild progenitors.

Taller varieties like the creamy 'Milky White ('Alba')', 'Purple Gleam' and 'Red Chief' at about 18 in./45 cm. are now available. They also appear in invaluable color-themed mixtures where, in spite of their height, they're often the first to flower.

Most recent improvements mirror the developments of the early years of the nineteenth century. Sutton's Seeds, in England, were the first, with dwarf varieties such as 'Sutton's Flame' as well as some with fluted petals like 'Sutton's Gaiety' and 'Sutton's Frilled Pink'. 'Sutton's Gaiety' was also very striking in its dramatic bicolored flowers; the insides of the flowers were pure white, the outside brilliant red. These have long since vanished and, with the present vogue for ever shorter varieties, are unlikely ever to return. However, we may well see these color combinations on dwarf plants – perhaps even with silver foliage.

Eschscholzia *'Rose Chiffon'*

The revival of the old fluted types is evident in the 'Thai Silk' mix with single flowers, while the flowers in the 'Ballerina' mix (sometimes called 'Prima Ballerina') are double, in various degrees. But it's the single colors which have made a mark in recent years and they are captivating.

The best varieties are those which combine silvery foliage and fluted flowers in various shades. The names include 'Apricot Bush', 'Apricot Chiffon', 'Apricot Flambeau', 'Rose Bush', 'Rose Chiffon',

and 'Sugared Almonds', although it has to be said that some of these may be synonyms (it's not clear which!) 'Rose Chiffon' is especially gorgeous. Its yellow eye lifts it from a familiar pink and silver pastel combination into something more special. That additional coloring makes it ideal to scatter in pale yellow and beige pea-gravel (rather than gray grit) – and that's all you need to do, scatter the seed. After the first rains the seed will germinate. The early silvery leaves look delightful against the pebbles from the moment they unfurl. 'Rose Chiffon' is also entrancing, emerging from the silver of *Lamium maculatum* 'White Nancy'.

I was amazed when 'Apricot Chiffon' sowed itself into the ground-hugging *Veronica reptans* 'Sunshine', whose flat carpet of yellow leaves (and absence of blue flowers) sneak slowly across gravel; this makes a stunning combination.

Rather different from all these is *Eschscholzia lobbii*, known colloquially in California as 'frying pans'. The plant reaches only 6 in./15 cm. and the flowers are the smallest of the cultivated eschscholzias, often just a quarter of the size of the California poppy, and bright yellow in color. It's superb for crevices in a sunny stone terrace. Trickle the seed along the cracks and it will soon be in flower. The rich yellow *E. caespitosa* is a bushy little species, large in growth and significantly larger in flower than *E. lobbii*. 'Sundew', its paler lemony form, will grow happily in the cracks of an old limestone wall where just enough seedlings should reappear each year to maintain the display.

LEFT *California poppies have an endearing ability to self-sow in the right places and this vegetable garden proves the point. Here, a few orange seedlings bring sparks of color among the cabbages, shallots and parsley, but unless deadheaded, or pulled out ruthlessly, they will cover the whole vegetable garden the following year.*

ABOVE RIGHT *California poppies like this 'Milky White', together with yellow forms closer to the wild type, are important constituents of yellow color-themed mixtures which are so valuable in new gardens. Here, the pale Calendula 'Lemon Pygmy' and a camissonia add to the blend.*

RIGHT Eschscholzia lobbii

Eucalyptus *Eucalyptus*

In the wild and in warm gardens, eucalyptus make enormous trees, some with spectacular flaking bark, shimmering silver foliage and spidery white, yellow or red flowers. It may sound as if they have no place in this book but the ability of a few species to reach 6 ft./1.8 m. in their first summer from seed is invaluable.

Back in the nineteenth century, eucalyptus were great favorites; in British seaside resorts of the 50s and 60s they reappeared as features in formal bedding schemes. Now they have new roles as valuable partners in contemporary mixed borders, as silver highlights both in Britain and North America and as ingredients in more informal summer annual plantings.

The blue gum, *Eucalyptus globulus*, with fat and strong stems and large, soft, blue-gray leaves, is outstanding. Sow it in spring at about 70°F/21°C, prick out first into 3 in./7 cm. pots then move on into 5 in./12.5 cm. pots or even larger ones. The crucial clue to growing a luxuriant specimen in the garden is not to let the roots become potbound before planting. This can easily happen if you sow the seed in winter in the hope of developing a substantial specimen for planting out – but the plant may become restricted in a small pot. In the coziness of the greenhouse,

growth of both shoots and roots is rapid; if the pot is too small the roots curl round inside. Then, after planting, the leafy top growth catches the wind like a sail and constantly loosens the roots which struggle to grow from their tightly curled rootball. Even if you knock in a stake for support, because it must be placed close to the stem, the stake ravages the root ball on its way to more solid soil below. A large pot, on the other hand, gives the roots space to develop freely in their early stages, prevents their becoming potbound and so allows them to grow out more freely after planting.

Eucalyptus are essential ingredients in the pastel, pink, and silver schemes still so popular. Try them with sweet peas, such as the striped lilac-and-white 'Lilac Ripple' or 'Anthea Turner' in rose-pink and cream, falling into them from a fence or wigwam of canes alongside or behind. Try them with the irresistible two-tone, pink and white *Salvia coccinea* 'Coral Nymph', tall enough to grow up into the lower branches; or with the pale lavender-rose *Petunia* 'Misty Lilac Wave', bred for hanging baskets and as ground cover but a great scrambler through the branches, given a little early help.

With blue too, *E. globulus* is special – and top of the list of companions must be 'Heavenly Blue' morning glory, in soft and silky sky blue; silver foliage is the perfect foil. Plant the morning glory at the base, check that it climbs the eucalyptus and refrains from surging off in another direction and it will look superb. *Ageratum* 'Blue Horizon', the blue and white *Salvia farinacea* 'Strata', and more silver in *Senecio cineraria* 'Silver Dust' can go around it.

LEFT *The blue gum,* Eucalyptus globulus, *is the most widely used eucalyptus for single-season effect. Here, it mingles with a specimen castor bean plant,* Ricinus 'Zanzibarensis'; *both reach over 6 ft./1.8 m. high in their first summer. To the left is the plant cataloged as "annual sugar cane", a form of* Sorghum vulgare, *which is striking in flower, and in front is the perennial* Eryngium pandanifolium *which in its second year makes a statuesque flowering plant.*

Eucalyptus gunnii

Gazania *Gazania*

Most gardeners would give gazanias rather a mixed reference. Undeniably colorful, their sparkling flowers have the unfortunate reputation of closing in dull weather – a reputation which, in the case of older varieties, is entirely deserved. This has led some gardeners simply to pass them by, turning to boring old marigolds when they need plants in this color range.

Two things have happened which should dissuade all but the most stubborn from this view. The first is that with the Talent Series we have plants with soft gray foliage so that even when the flowers are closed the plants still have great value.

The second event of significance in the development of seed-raised gazanias is that a plant breeder in California started visiting his gazania trials in the middle of the night. This was not a sign that in his quest for the ever-open gazania he had finally abandoned control of his own reason – on the contrary.

In their native South Africa, gazania flowers close up in poor weather to protect the pollen from moisture. This mechanism is triggered by low temperatures, poor light or by a combination of the two. Older varieties like 'Sunshine', 'Sundance', and 'Harlequin' were effective outside only in bright sunny weather and, on the rare occasions when they were brought into the house as cut flowers, the constant warmth ensured the flowers remained open. Plant breeders have been working intensively on developing gazanias in which this mechanism is less prominent, allowing the flowers to stay open longer in cooler, duller climates.

Visiting the gazania trials in the middle of the night revealed individual plants which closed up a little bit less than their neighbors. These were then checked during day-light hours, and the best plants were then incorporated into the breeding program. The result was the Daybreak Series, whose flowers really do stay open longer than other gazanias.

'Daybreak Red Stripe' is especially startling, recalling the best of 'Sundance' and 'Harlequin' in its boldly striped flowers, but with the addition of a newly introduced long flowering habit. It makes an impressive planting with the cuttings-raised *Oenothera* 'African Sun' alongside, or *Bidens* 'Golden Eye'; it's important to plant gazanias with low-growing neighbors as they flower so much less well when overshadowed.

The color range has broadened too, although I see little point in the pinks and cream which have now appeared in the Chansonette and Mini-Star series; they always look slightly dirty. The more familiar yellows, orange shades, chestnut, and gold, in some cases striped in contrasting shades or with contrasting marks at the base of the petals, are far more effective and appealing.

Although gazanias make splendid mixers in sunny containers and in intimate plantings in small sunny corners, they also make spectacular ground cover. On sunny banks along the drive or at the front of a property facing a road, sweeps of 'Talent' gazanias may cause passing drivers to swerve in shock and astonishment – so avoid this planting if you live on a bend.

Gazania x hybrida *'Mini Star'*

Gazania *'Talent'*

RIGHT *The fiery tones of Gazania 'Sundance' on trial at Unwin's Seeds in Cambridgeshire, England. Most of the larger seed companies worldwide hold trials where they not only assess potential new introductions, but grow the same seed as they put in the packets as a quality control.*

Godetia Godetia

North American natives they may be, but godetias have made an unjustifiably minimal impact on North American gardeners. The fact that they're so often referred to as clarkias, when in truth most clarkias are more correctly known as godetias, only serves to confuse the issue. But although it still requires a certain diligence to track down any but the occasional mixture, believe me it's worth going to some trouble to search them out.

Godetias have two special qualities. The satiny sheen on their petals is unrivalled; even on dull days it shimmers and flickers, and as you look into the flower with its slender stamens and divided style, it's as if a ballroom dancer had fallen on her bottom and kicked her legs in the air (allowing for some license in the details of human anatomy). And godetias come in such colors – no yellows and no genuine blues, it's true, but among the purples, reds, pinks, and white there's a unity of tone which allows even the mixtures to harmonize. There are also some unique colors and bicolors and all are very easy to grow.

Like nasturtiums, which have suffered from much the same tainted reputation, godetias were once very popular in England and available in a wide range of colors. In the 1880s Suttons Seeds listed 10 varieties, in the 1920s it was up to 23 and even in the 1950s British catalogs listed between 10 and 20 varieties. Then they declined; by the 1980s many catalogs listed but three or four. Now a revival is taking shape and single colors are occasionally appearing in American catalogs.

Godetia *'Salmon Princess'*

Godetia *'Schamini Rose'*

The revival began with the F_1 hybrid Grace Series of tall cut-flower types which are exceptionally prolific and come in seven separate colors; they're superb in borders with perennials or as cut flowers for display in the house and can produce 15 stems per plant. Cut them when about a third of the flowers on the stem are open and the remainder will open in the vase.

The dwarf, eight-color Satin Series followed. These plants are incredibly prolific with some gorgeous individual colors, but in some catalogs the seed is over 200 times the price of older varieties! Its arrival increased interest in godetias but less in these expensive F_1 hybrids and more in the old types. 'Sybil Sherwood', in salmon orange with a white edge, is perhaps the only old variety which never quite disappeared. Now 'Salmon Princess' has returned, the tall, semi-double 'Schamini' type has been recently reintroduced, and individual colors such as 'Rembrandt' in red with a white edge and 'Duke of York' in carmine with a white center have come back.

Mixtures like 'Bornita' and 'Improved Dwarf' have been upgraded, new introductions like 'Precious Gems', which is blended from individual colors, have taken the mixtures to new heights . . . everything is looking up for the godetia. Except that the botanists have scrapped the name and merged them into the clarkias; catalogs still list them as godetias, and so do I.

In the garden, single colors like 'Salmon Princess' and 'Schamini Carmine' fit well into mixed plantings with

perennials and can be sown as late as early summer and still flower well. Interplanted or backed with forms of *Salvia coccinea* and taller forms of *Salvia farinacea*, the effect is striking and the contrast in flower forms very appealing.

The unusually speedy Satin Series can even be sown direct to follow sweet Williams, which are usually still at their peak at planting time for summer bedding.

ABOVE *The bronze-purple foliage of* Heuchera *'Palace Purple' makes the perfect companion for a plant from* Godetia *'Improved Dwarf Mixed'. Individual plants were raised in pots and planted in the most appropriate places in the border when the first godetia flowers showed their color.*

Helianthus *Sunflower*

In 1888 Vincent Van Gogh was living in Provence, in the Yellow House at Arles, and during the summer of that year he painted a series of pictures of orchards, gardens, and sunflowers and used them to decorate the house for the visit of Paul Gauguin. He wanted this decoration to create "effects like those of a stained-glass window in a Gothic church."

During this time he looked forward to a new life in which people would "live in nature as though they were flowers". The symbolic sunflower came to represent Van Gogh's conviction that an artistic renaissance could only take place in the sun.

For the gardener, even the briefest look at his vibrant sunflower pictures reveals something unexpected. Few flowers arranged in that familiar cream and yellow vase resemble today's idea of a typical sunflower. The ray florets of some are slim and shaggy, in others they've almost vanished and the flowers resemble fat orange buns.

European catalogs from the late 1880s show few such variants. There's a tall single yellow, a primrose yellow single new in 1889, a dwarf form reaching about 3 ft./90 cm., a tall double orange, and a shorter, well-branched, small-flowered form. Those shown in Van Gogh's paintings were probably grown in gardens from home-saved seed where variations would often occur or, perhaps as likely, the plants raised from bought seed were inherently variable.

Since then, the color range has widened. There are more doubles like 'Orange Sun', shorter varieties suitable for small gardens and for cutting have appeared and so-called 'pollen free' types, which don't shed pollen on the furniture when cut for the house, have also been introduced. Among those in

unusual colors, the tall 'Velvet Queen' is a deep and sumptuous velvety reddish brown at its best, but in my garden has proved variable. 'Prado Red', sometimes called 'Ruby Sunset', is more uniform in color and, at 4–6 ft./1.2–1.8 m., a little shorter. 'Valentine' is a lovely creamy yellow with a black disk and 'Moonwalker' has attractively branched, pale heads with rather a frilly look.

There are still relatively few doubles and some are less than immediately appealing. 'Teddy Bear' reaches about 2 ft./60 cm. with yellow, rayless pincushion flowers. The rather gross 'Sungold' with big double flowers on 6–8 ft./1.8–2.4 m. stems is also occasionally listed. Dwarf types are slowly becoming more widely available. 'Holiday' reaches 4 ft./1.2 m. and branches strongly from the base. It was bred for cutting but also makes a wonderful border plant, especially with dark-stemmed *Aster lateriflorus* crowding in alongside. In a container, 'Elf' keeps to just 15 in./38 cm; 'Pacino' can be even smaller.

In gardens, the taller sunflowers make a superb screen around the vegetable garden, or to divide it; 'Valentine', 'Prado Red' or 'Chianti', and 'Prado Yellow' would be ideal. Along new boundaries they can make a spectacular show. If space allows, grow three or four varieties, one behind the other. If not, a row of 'Valentine' or 'Pastiche' mixture could go at the back with 'Teddy Bear' or 'Music Box' mix in front. In mixed borders 'Moonwalker', 'Velvet Queen', or 'Sunbeam' are an elegant back-of-the-border presence, especially in the first year after planting when tall perennials may not make their full height. However, even in later seasons their color and poise reliably continue to give full value.

Helianthus *'Velvet Queen'*

Helianthus *'Orange Sun'*

LEFT *Dwarf sunflowers can be difficult to integrate into mixed plantings, but by careful choice of variety and of neighboring plants you can create attractive combinations. Here, 'Pacino' is set against the slender foliage of Bowles' golden grass,* Milium effusum *'Aureum', while in front are two almost perfectly matching annuals. Viola 'Universal Primrose Shades' has a slightly darker lip but the upper petals match almost exactly the crinkled flowers of the 'Primrose Gem' nasturtiums. The broad, bold leaves of 'Bull's Blood' ornamental beet fill the foreground with contrasting deep bronze.*

Helichrysum *Strawflower*

Best known as attractive, 'everlasting' dried flowers (wire the stems to keep the heads from drooping), helichrysums are strangely neglected as fresh cut flowers and as annuals for summer borders. But their color range is now unexpectedly impressive and the newer, taller types with up to twelve separate colors come in intriguing pastels as well as the old-style fiery shades.

All, naturally, keep their color for an unusually long time and, in habit, many fit with perennials especially well. Only the relative difficulty in finding the separate colors with which to plan effective plant associations has held them back; now, this is being remedied.

Although strawflowers are tough enough to be sown outside in many areas, treating them as half-hardy annuals and raising them in pots is more dependable and ensures earlier flowering. This technique is especially useful with plants chosen from the newer, taller types with their wider range of colors, such as the King Size and Sultane series. Raising them in pots, finishing at 5 in./12.5 cm., allows you to position them more precisely in border plantings.

For many years 'Bright Bikinis' were the only dwarf type and, at first, made good bedders; 'Hot Bikini' in fiery orange red was the only widely available separate color and this certainly looked the part with beetroot, 'Malibu' lettuce, or other reddish foliage. But seed stocks deteriorated and the plants seemed taller each time I grew them. Now the invaluable Chico Series in five colors is supplanting them and although plants can be rather squat they have the advantage of spreading surpisingly well. The seed is more expensive than that of 'Bright Bikinis' so you'll find far less in the packets, although the quality is far more dependable.

Oh, finally, just one more thing: helichrysums may seem inexplicably absent from some reference books. The truth is that the botanists now place them in the genus *Bracteantha* – try there. The various forms of the licorice plant, *Helichrysum petiolare*, silvery relations of the strawflowers, remain helichrysums.

LEFT *'Chico White', one of five colors in the dwarfest series yet seen, sits neatly among 'Lemon Gem' marigolds with 'Malibu' lettuce in the background. For the more intimate tapestry plantings the Chico Series is ideal, although when grown in poor soil it can look depressingly dumpy; rich conditions and no lack of water give it a slightly more open and uneven look. I've found that regular deadheading prolongs the flowering season significantly.*

Hesperis *Sweet Rocket*

"Among the most desirable of hardy flowers," wrote William Robinson in *The English Flower Garden* in 1883. Well, sweet rocket, sometimes called dame's violet, is indeed delightful, and desirable, especially the white form, *Hesperis matronalis* var. *albiflora,* which has a purity of color that makes it invaluable both as a tall, informal ingredient of spring bedding schemes (with *Allium* 'Purple Sensation' – wow!) and as a dependable self-seeding woodlander.

Sweet rocket's endearingly relaxed habit of growth, which fits well into mixed borders of all kinds, is useful not only in shady sites, where it's most often seen, but in sunnier sites too. Flowering as it does in early summer, its clouds of small flowers are perfect if they are allowed to self-sow among the strong shapes of interplanted Oriental poppies and bearded irises. With self-sown 'Mother of Pearl' poppies, it can fill a whole border with refreshing color.

This combination works exceptionally well, especially if sweet rocket is restricted to the white form – when the mauve appears alongside some Oriental poppies and irises, the resultant color combinations can be a little too disputatious. Carefully choosing varieties of poppy and iris creates more comfortable groupings with the mauve form; white, pink and purple are more suitable than orange, scarlet and bright yellow.

Apart from the purity of its white and the softness of its mauve coloring, its other irresistible quality is the scent – it is, after all, called sweet rocket. (This name derives from a comparison with rocket, or roquette, the salad vegetable, which does not have sweetly scented flowers. It also goes by the mysterious name of "close sciences"!)

As evening falls, the scent of the sweet rocket is powerful and soft, intoxicating in the best sense of the word. Just a few plants bring fragrance enough to a small garden.

LEFT *In woodland situations, white sweet rocket,* Hesperis matronalis var. albiflora *is perfectly at home, often naturalizing, its clean white flowers bringing light to shady borders. Here it makes a bright combination with the freshly unfurled fronds of the shuttlecock fern,* Matteuccia struthiopteris. *Sweet rocket has relatively sparse foliage so hellebores, winter aconites and other early flowers growing underneath will not be smothered.*

Impatiens *Impatiens*

The first I saw of impatiens (in Britain, they're known, strangely as busy lizzies) was in the damp light of an early summer morning in the London suburbs. A huge plant filled the window of a Victorian house where, as a kid, I delivered newspapers, its clay pot tottering on the inside windowsill. Bare stems were its most striking feature, the leaves were sparse and pale and the scattering of brash pink flowers seemed insufficient to redeem the situation. When it disappeared, I noticed a few stray leaves peeping out of the trash can. I then forgot about impatiens for ten years.

Now the impatiens, as it's mostly called, is the best-selling bedding plant in the world, transformed by plant breeders, for both better and worse, into a dwarf and prolific plant which tolerates a wide variety of conditions, especially shade. In rich soil and plenty of moisture, plants develop an open, companionable habit which suits the intimate, intermingling schemes which are ideal in today's small gardens. Neglected, and in poor soil, an inelegant tightness of habit reduces their appeal.

The familiar bedding impatiens can be difficult to tell apart: the Expo, Tempo, Super Elfin, and Accent series include more than twenty different colors each and the nuance in shades can be very useful when planning small-scale plantings with the precision and care they deserve.

There are also two interesting smaller series. The Swirls,

Impatiens *'Bruno White'*

Impatiens *'Mosaic Lilac'*

Impatiens glandulifera *'Candida'*

which partner the Super Elfins, are delightful with their dark picotee edges to the paler flowers; the two Mosaic colors have a delicate patterning of speckles which may not show up well in mass bedding but is truly captivating in containers.

The best advice is to scour the catalogs for separate colors which exactly suit the effects you wish to create. Mixtures, as usual, predominate, but don't buy them. There are twenty-seven colors in the 'Tempo' mixture and 40 seeds in a packet; what are the chances of actually getting one plant in each color? Combine red, orange, purple, pinks of all kinds and cerise (some with white starry patterns) in one bed and the result can be spectacular . . . spectacularly lurid. But from so many nuanced colors some wonderful color-themed blends have been created. 'Super Elfin Mother of Pearl' is the pick, a meld of pastel pinks, lilacs and white which is outstanding and, as impatiens thrive in moist shade, can bring true light to the darker areas of smaller city gardens. In brighter sites with silver foliage like *Senecio cineraria* 'Cirrus' or the compact form of *Helichrysum petiolare*, these soft shades seem almost fashionable again.

The Bruno Series has brought unexpected benefits for the home gardener: the seeds are larger than those of other impatiens and the seedlings more vigorous, making them easier to handle. The plants are also more open in habit, the flowers larger, and both petals and foliage thicker, so they do better in hotter, drier conditions than other varieties.

Of course, there are other annual impatiens. New Guinea impatiens have become increasingly popular but these are sun worshipers, without a doubt (although they appreciate lots of water). In the cooler Northwest they're less successful but, where they can be sure of summer heat and no shortage of moisture, they can be spectacular. 'Tango Improved', with deep orange flowers, will reach up to 2 ft./60 cm. and looks great in front of dark-leaved cannas. The shorter Spectra Series, in a mix and five separate colors, has variegated foliage to add to the display.

Another variety which has caused a stir in cooler areas, mainly for the wrong reasons, is *Impatiens glandulifera*, the Himalayan balsam. The succulent seedlings germinate by the thousand and soon smother their neighbors; the result is that this tall, moisture-loving, purplish-flowered species can become a pest in damp places. I have to say, though, that the white form, 'Candida' is especially beautiful.

The bedding impatiens are trickier to raise and are best sown at about 70°F/21°C but certainly no warmer than 75°F/23°C. They germinate best with some light; this does not mean full sun, rather that a dusting of vermiculite as a covering is more suitable than a sifting of seed starting mix. Never water seeds or seedlings with cold water.

Cover the seed pot with plastic wrap to keep the seeds moist and, after pricking out, avoid sudden fluctuations in temperature (especially cold spells); plants which have endured this interrupted growth develop unevenly with a mix of short and long shoots and may not establish well once planted.

RIGHT *Using a mixture of plants in different colors needs careful thought. Here, although there are nine different genera in and around this terra-cotta chimney-pot, the color range is sufficiently restricted to ensure harmony. Impatiens 'Accent White' is close in color to the pale edges of the pansy flowers, the light tips of* Helichrysum petiolare *'Limelight', the variegated ivy and felicia, and also the pale lime nicotiana flowers. The lobelia, petunia, and dark pansy are all in the same color range so the contrast with the impatiens and other pale colors is a soft one.*

Ipomoea *Morning Glory*

Sorry, I must sit down . . . it makes me go weak just to think about the silky sheen on those delicate petals . . . like caressing . . . . 'Heavenly Blue' ipomoea is essential; no one with a soul can resist it once seen. Like the most captivating of lovers it's not perfect but is nevertheless both irresistible and deeply satisfying – the perfect combination.

This may all seem a little excessive. But to see those buds poised in the afternoon sun, rolled like strange sea mollusks, ready to unfurl the next day before even the photographer deputed to record them is awake and out in the garden in the best of the first light . . . . They have so much allure with so little pretension. Confidently gorgeous in the privacy of the best light, in the suffocating heat of the day they close up and there's nothing to see – except tomorrow's potential.

'Heavenly Blue' is the best, but its growth depends on the summer weather. Given warmth it will thrive, even in a short season, luxuriating and flourishing, covering fences with foliage and exquisite flowers. In cooler gardens or seasons, growth is less rapid, especially in the early stages when the foliage and growth tips may develop yellow streaks; this is a plant whose response to warmth is striking.

There are other shades in this group, based on *Ipomoea tricolor* and *I. nil*, but they need more warmth. Many of these are descendants of the Imperial morning glories which gripped Japan in the mid-nineteenth century in much the same way that tulipomania swept Europe. As much as eight dollars per seed is known to have been paid by the lustful and avaricious.

Japanese catalogs still list an unexpectedly wide range of unusual ipomoeas; few are listed in the West, although 'Chocolate', in a strange milk chocolate shade with a dash of rose, is sometimes seen. Doubles such as 'Double Blue Picotee', the 'Early Call' mixture in scarlet, white, orange, pink, and purple, and the repulsive 'Roman Candy' with its white splotched leaves (which I cannot discuss further) tend to require warmer conditions even than 'Heavenly Blue'. In many areas they are more dependable as sunroom or greenhouse plants – red spider mite will probably ruin them, but not before you've enjoyed them for a few weeks.

There is also a group of hardier sorts based on *I. purpurea*, once known as *Convolvulus major*. Sow these outside where they're to flower ('Heavenly Blue' and its allies may need an indoor start). They are usually only available in an irritating mixture including purple, pink, red, cerise, and white, although separate colors are occasionally listed. These include what purports to be *I. purpurea* the species, 'Crimson Rambler' in more of a cerise color with a clear white eye, the brighter 'Scarlet O'Hara', and the best, the wonderfully rich and vivid 'Grandpa Otts' which is both dependably leafy and prolific. Grow this, or the very similar 'Star of Yelta', up through a dark buddleja such as 'Black Knight' for a uniquely sultry display.

Ipomoea purpurea

Ipomoea *'Double Blue Picotee'*

RIGHT Ipomoea 'Mini Sky-blue' is only slightly smaller in flower than 'Heavenly Blue' but is certainly less vigorous in growth. This allows it to be sprawled on the ground to twine through its neighbors, in this case Salvia farinacea 'Blue Victory', without smothering them, and its tempting trumpets spark joyful surprise. Its tendency to develop creamy marks in cool conditions, which can just be seen here, is the more easily masked when it snakes among leafy neighbors.

Lathyrus Sweet Pea

Sweet peas have been the subject of oscillating fashions over the years yet, while they may not have quite regained the extraordinary popularity they once enjoyed, sweet peas are the one annual which non-gardeners love and which even prejudiced gardeners exclude from their otherwise sweeping derision directed against annuals generally.

The intoxicating fragrance of sweet peas, at its most penetrating on warm dry days, delights everyone from reminiscing grandmothers for whom the sweet pea inspires powerful, if rather vague, warm nostalgia to toddlers simply surprised by the scent. Bees and pollen beetles like them too. It's especially refreshing that enthusiasm for sweet peas not only extends across the whole wide spectrum of gardeners but also encompasses almost the whole range of styles of sweet peas themselves, from wild species and old varieties to the latest introductions.

Whole books have been written on the chronological history of sweet peas, but let me summarize. The wild sweet pea, *Lathyrus odoratus*, originates in Malta and was sent by the monk Franciscus Cupani to England in 1699. This was probably the magenta and purple bicolor we now grow as 'Cupani'; its scent is overpowering, the colors rich but the flowers small. By 1800 five colors had appeared including, in 1726, 'Painted Lady', the pretty pink-and white bicolor which still looks so good twining up through *Lavatera* 'Barnsley' with its attractive pink-centered, white flowers.

Towards the end of the nineteenth century there were two leaps forward. Henry Eckford, from Shropshire, England, developed the Grandiflora sweet peas, with (comparatively speaking) larger flowers, in a better shape and a wider range of colors, which still retain the fragrance, strength, and free-flowering style of their predecessors.

Although neglected for decades the remarkable fragrance of these Grandifloras has again made them increasingly popular at a time when more modern types are less dependable in their perfume. They're also used to make up mixtures with names like 'Old Spice' and 'Old Fashioned Scented Mixed'. There are even new types in this group available from England, such as the white 'Vanilla Ice' and the scarlet 'Philip Miller' with its blue flecks. All are best grown where their relatively small flowers can be appreciated: by a gate or on one side of a doorway where the scent will waft through tantalizingly to the other side.

In 1901, everything changed. In three different gardens the pink Grandiflora 'Prima Donna', one of Henry Eckford's most popular introductions, sported a new flower form. It happened with Henry's own plants, it happened in the cut-flower nursery of William Unwin near Cambridge and it happened at Countess Spencer's family home at Althorp in Northamptonshire (now well known as the childhood home of Princess Diana). In all three places, sports appeared with much larger flowers, a more open shape and with a noticeable wave in the standard (the upright part of the flower). The Althorp type was introduced by head gardener Silas Cole as 'Countess Spencer' but proved rather variable; the slightly smaller-flowered Unwin's type was introduced as 'Gladys Unwin' and was much more uniform. The two came together as the Spencer sweet peas.

Sweet peas in this style are the most widely grown today but a few years before the first Spencers appeared, in California in 1894, a very

Lathyrus odoratus *'Sunsilk'*

Lathyrus odoratus *'Helen Thomas'*

RIGHT *Training sweet peas on a wigwam of 8 ft./2.4 m. bamboo canes is the simplest way to grow them for cutting. Push the canes at least 2 ft./60 cm. into the ground and tie them securely at the top. The whole mass of stems should also be tied in loosely as they develop, or they may collapse away from their support – as they're showing signs of starting to do here. Set against the dark green of the yew, this colorful mixture stands out well, although a color coordinated blend such as 'Rosemary Verey' in pinks and cream, would blend more happily with the delphiniums alongside than this multicolored mix. Although flowers will be picked for the house from this planting, it will still look well in the flower border as there should still be plenty of bloom to give a bright display in the garden.*

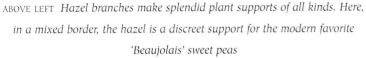

ABOVE LEFT *Hazel branches make splendid plant supports of all kinds. Here, in a mixed border, the hazel is a discreet support for the modern favorite 'Beaujolais' sweet peas*

ABOVE RIGHT *Long straight, newly-cut hazel poles are bent into an arch and the flat, fan-like tip growth is used to fill the gaps around the sides, the better to support the old-fashioned 'Cupani' sweet peas. This looks elegant from the moment it's set up and, as the sweet peas continue to clamber up, its character still shows through.*

different type was discovered: a small-flowered, very dwarf, slightly spreading variety christened 'Cupid'. Like the Grandifloras, this too all but disappeared but has now been revived to the extent that pots of 'Cupid' are sold in garden centers for planting in windowboxes.

Over the years other dwarf types have appeared, though none quite so remarkably prostrate as 'Cupid'. The 2–3 ft./60–90 cm. 'Snoopea' mixture is probably the best known. Its silly name may have deterred as many gardeners as it attracted. It has no tendrils, unlike the 3 ft./90 cm. 'Jet Set'; this is admirably self-supporting but sadly no longer available in the delightful separate colors as it once was. More recently, 'Explorer' has appeared, a non-tendril type with seven colors in a brighter, sharper color mix than the eight more pastel shades of 'Jet Set'.

New colors and color combinations have also been added to the Spencer sweet peas. The flowers have become larger, with a greater certainty of individual stems carrying four or five flowers but they're less dependably scented; some are hardly scented at all. Other recent developments have included some striking bicolors from New Zealand known as 'Bicolor Melody' or sometimes 'Romance', 'Love Match', 'Hammett Bicolors', or 'Kiwi Bicolor Mixed'. Striped varieties have returned, first as 'Unwins Mixed Stripes', then in the Ripple Series, then in the Heavenly Series, and soon in 'Rosy Dawn', the first striped version of a Spencer sweet pea with orange-red patterning on white. 'Helen Thomas' is a striking picotee, 'Sunsilk' a shimmering orange-pink.

Most seed breeders who specialize in sweet peas concentrate on the Spencer varieties, and there's an increasing feeling among non-specialist gardeners that new introductions are too similar to earlier varieties. The seed breeder's urge to introduce *something* new every year often overwhelms the necessity to ensure that new introductions are genuine improvements. This has prompted a wariness of new varieties and an inclination to look back to older types, even to wild species.

Wild types other than those derived from *Lathyrus odoratus* have increasingly been employed. Forms of *L. tingitanus* with unexpectedly large flowers in shades of red and pink, as well as bicolors, are ideal growing through cistus or brooms in Mediterranean-style plantings. *Lathyrus chloranthus*, with greeny-yellow flowers on vigorous plants, makes you gasp as it sprawls through one of the Mediterranean euphorbias such as *E. characias*.

Growing sweet peas is easy to do badly. Sweet peas will survive and flower from a sowing at almost any time and in most conditions; but to thrive they need sunshine, rich soil, plenty of water, and regular attention to either picking the flowers or deadheading. Sow them in pots in fall and keep them through the winter before planting outside in spring and you will have the most robust, longest-flowering plants. This applies to all types.

ABOVE *'Cupid' is a variety from the late nineteenth century, revived and reintroduced almost a hundred years later. It grows to no more than a few inches or centimeters in height and spreads to no more than 9 in./23 cm. across, its pretty two-tone flowers appearing over a long period all summer. Here, it creeps over blue-stained edging boards from under an old cuttings-raised coleus, 'Rob Roy'. A few silvery wands of Plecostachys serpyllifolia, sometimes called petite licorice plant, peep into the top of the picture.*

Lavatera **Mallow**

The satiny sheen on the petals of a mallow is unique among annuals: sheer and tempting, open to delicate caress, apparently fragile but reassuringly tough – like a flapper out on a date. Few annuals mix such allure with such easy availability!

That sheen combines with the constant profusion of flower – and a good price – to bring us one of the most valuable of all annuals – and one which has shown how a neglected species can be improved. The naming could be improved too – bush mallow, tree mallow, mallow, or lavatera – everyone seems to call them something different.

'Silver Cup' showed what could be achieved by careful selection in what had been a relatively undeveloped species. In addition to their tactile quality, the petals are broad and overlap to create a more substantial flower. The markings on the petals are bolder and more distinct and there are more flowers on each stem than in older types.

And 'Silver Cup' was the right plant at the right time. Mixed borders had become commonplace, yet the short and bushy annuals which were still the norm looked out of place in such plantings; the two styles of plants looked uncomfortable together. 'Silver Cup' had not only the quality but also the stature and the style to look well alongside, say, *Aster* x *frikartii* 'Mönch', or attractive in front of a

Lavatera *'White Cherub'*

Lavatera *'Silver Cup'*

silvery elaeagnus or pyrus, or behind the crowded glaucous stems of autumn sedums. So it was an instant success; annuals which associate well with shrubs and hardy perennials are invaluable.

In succeeding years additional varieties appeared occasionally: 'Mont Blanc', white, with exceptionally dark foliage and its pink counterpart 'Mont Rose'; 'Ruby Regis' in carmine pink; then more recently the Beauty Series in two veined pinks, white and a carmine; then the even more prolific 'White Cherub', shorter and a little more crowded in the flower head but retaining its ability to integrate.

Another feature of lavateras which has enabled them to fit well into changing styles of gardening is their adaptability. They can be raised as hardy annuals, sown directly, and thinned to about 12 in./30 cm.; they can also be raised indoors and pricked out into pots or even trays; and they can recover from a period of poor growing conditions and still give a good display.

Recently, however, a problem has arisen. Lavatera leaf-spot disease first attacks plants at ground level and then attacks the foliage, causing plants to collapse unexpectedly and dramatically – ruining the display. Most commercial seed is treated against the disease if it's found when tested by the seed company; plants grown from home-saved seed are more vulnerable.

RIGHT *Color-themed mixtures can include a wide, if unpredictable, range of varieties, in a narrow color range and here among the pink-flowered mixture, the salmon and rose shades are flowering together.* Lavatera 'Pink Beauty' *dominates; the color is simply so powerful. The rosy bracts of a pink* Salvia viridis *pick up the same shade while* Clarkia 'Apple Blossom' *fills in delicately behind the bold pods of the sometimes banned opium poppy* Papaver somniferum *– whose flowers are more fleeting but which clearly have other attractions.*

Linaria Toadflax

An old favorite and a series of impressive newcomers are bringing linarias to new prominence in the annual border, rescuing them from their former obscurity. In the cool-summer zones it prefers, *Linaria purpurea* has often been treated almost as a weed. Its particular purple coloring is not a sympathetic one and it self-seeds all too determinedly. The rose-pink 'Canon Went' redeems its reputation in bucketfuls, and the slightly shorter 'Springside White' is also proving valuable. Both flower well in their first year from seed and their slender spikes add a bold upright accent to mixed borders and spacious annual plantings.

But now, from Japan, comes the Fantasia (or Fantasy) Series. Like mimulus, they can flower in as little as six weeks from sowing. They then develop dense clouds of tiny flowers which, although carried on short plants, nevertheless retain a charm lacking in so many dwarf varieties. They meld well with shorter annual phlox, impatiens, and silver-leaved licorice plants.

Eventually, the flowers fade. The kitchen scissors then have a job to do, snipping the whole plant back by half. A precautionary soak with liquid fertilizer, perhaps another soak from the watering can if the weather is dry, and they soon burst into flower again. Unfortunately seed of Fantasia is very expensive so it's best to raise it in pots where there will be fewer losses. But it's worth the extra cost.

Seed of traditional annual linarias, such as the 'Fairy Lights' mixture, is cheap and comes in vast quantities so you can sow it outside where it's to flower. These older linarias come only in mixtures, but in gaps or cracks in paving they can be delightful; and the color range can be manipulated by purposeful deadheading. New, in a similar style comes 'Gemstones'. Its grayish foliage and slightly floppy growth carry a succession of long-spurred flowers in red and orange shades. Ideal in a small sunny container, being a perennial it will flower again early in its second year, as long as its roots are not left too sodden in the winter.

LEFT *At Nori and Sandra Pope's garden at Hadspen House in Somerset, England, the familiar* Linaria purpurea *'Canon Went' is an invaluable feature of the long border. Although a true perennial, this flowers prolifically in its first summer and here blends with the foliage of red orach and the vibrant* Dianthus carthusianorum *in the foreground. The linaria is a rampant self-seeder; even dedicated deadheading will leave a few seeds to produce seedlings next year.*

Lobelia Lobelia

For most gardeners there's only one species of annual lobelia, *Lobelia erinus*. Within this species there may be two types for different uses, the bushy for bedding and the trailing for baskets, but both are in decline. Yet it would be a shortsighted gardener who accepted this sad fact and simply let lobelia stagnate; there's scope for some creative planting here. Fortunately, I've found a new way of growing them for bedding and there's also a relatively unrecognized group of varieties deserving our wider attention.

Traditionally, bushy lobelia has been grown as an edging plant around formal bedding schemes, while trailing lobelia has been grown in hanging baskets, windowboxes and other containers. The dividing line has always been a strict one but I've always found 'Crystal Palace Compacta', 'Mrs. Clibran', and the other bushy bedding types rather contrary: they're too dumpy and squat yet they often collapse in heavy rain. So I tried planting trailing varieties like 'Blue Cascade' on the ground, and the result was a much lighter, more airy look. The lobelia intermingled attractively with neighboring plants and created an easy blend with the natural informality of perennials and relaxed annuals.

The older Cascade and Basket series are genuinely lax in habit, but the more recent Regatta Series is far superior. The plants branch more determinedly from the base, growth is a little more dense, there are fewer wispy trails and the whole plant seems to remain a little less unfocused. The result is a series of eight colors which are ideal for informal summer schemes and which also bring an increased

Lobelia 'Red Cascade' with Symphytum 'Goldsmith'

richness and denseness of color to baskets and containers.

What's more, a glittering new color appeared as part of the Regatta Series – a blue and white bicolor. This is simply spectacular; it is sparkling, light, and far more effective than other new shades such as the watery lilacs. *Lobelia* 'Regatta Blue Splash' planted in the ground with blue, white, and other blue-and-white bicolored flowers will bring you up with a start. Try a blend of 'Regatta Blue Splash', *Salvia farinacea* 'Strata', *Ageratum* 'Southern Cross' or 'Capri', with 'Mini Sky-blue' morning glory twisting through and the occasional cool pool of silver foliage.

Lobelia mixtures are a disaster. Now that there are up to eight different colors in a mix, color compatibility has become an issue. Blending together dark and light blues, white plus various carmine and washed-out lilac shades creates a peculiarly offensive result. Seed companies should formulate the colors into two mixtures: a combination of all the blue shades plus white, and a mix of the carmine, rosy and lilac shades plus white. Both would be valuable in different situations and indeed would make attractive baskets without the need for other companions.

The Regatta Series of bushy trailers and the "splash" type in both the Regatta and the ball-shaped Riviera Series have been significant recent improvements in lobelias; the other has been the development of F_1 hybrid *perennial* lobelias which are making an increasing impact as summer annuals.

The great breakthrough was the F_1 hybrid Compliment Series, now in three separate colors (the mix has additional shades). This was

LEFT *Seed-raised perennial lobelias, like this* Lobelia *'Queen Victoria', develop quickly enough to make a first-season impression. Here, in front of the rich yet sparkling blue flowers of* Salvia guaranitica *'Blue Enigma', the lobelia brings the eye forward from the fading sanguisorba in the background and its beetroot foliage sets off the blue salvia flowers well.*

RIGHT *White baskets are cool in every respect. Here,* Lobelia *'White Cascade' mingles in a simple planting with* Impatiens *'Accent White' to make a basket which is both soft and neat in its appearance. This corner site is ideal; both plants will do well – in fact, they probably grow best – in a little shade. White lobelia never comes 100% white, hence the few blue flowers from a single rogue plant.*

bred primarily as a cut flower, with 3 ft./90 cm. unbranched stems produced in good numbers – four is common in the first summer. The shorter Fan Series followed, in five colors; the plants branch from the base to produce an astonishing number of spikes just five months from sowing.

The pick of these are 'Compliment Scarlet' and 'Fan Scarlet' – the latter with strongly red-tinted foliage. As yet there's no white in either series and none with the beetroot-colored foliage seen in vegetatively propagated varieties. These plants are superb as first-year flowerers for the new perennial border, and for areas of summer annual planting schemes where an impact is required from a tall, upright plant which retains a little elegance. Try 'Fan Scarlet' with *Nicotiana langsdorffii* alongside and a billowing of *Delphinium* 'Snow Cloud' around them both, plus *Convolvulus* 'Red Ensign' in front with coleus 'Red Velvet' and *Nemesia* 'Innocence'.

There's yet another reason for growing these seed-raised perennial lobelias. Not only do they flower prolifically as annuals, but many vegetatively propagated perennial lobelias are badly infected with virus, so the seed-raised types, which do not carry virus infection, are becoming indispensable.

Raising lobelia from seed can be a tricky business for many gardeners. At 25,000 per gram the seeds really are minute; they're difficult to sow, the seedlings are tiny, they have a tendency to damp off, and they're very tricky to handle singly when

it comes to pricking out. The standard recommendation is to prick out in patches of seedlings – which are easier to handle. With mixtures this ensures you achieve a well-integrated blend of colors, and you will always find plenty of seeds in the packet – as many as 2,500.

But this is bad practice in two groups. White-flowered bedding lobelias always carry a small percentage of blue-flowered plants, which can ruin a carefully planned display. If you prick out seedlings singly you can eliminate any blues before planting. And packets of the Compliment and Fan series may contain as few as fifty seeds which, allowing for the inevitable loss of many tiny seedlings, can leave you with all too few. The answer is to sow all lobelias very thinly, at a minimum of 70°F/20°C, keep the seed moist, cover very lightly, and allow the seedlings to remain in the seed pot a little longer than usual; then they will be large enough to handle individually.

Lobularia Sweet Alyssum

People can be so unfair. Just because alyssum seed is usually cheap, and because it's so easy to grow, and because it self-seeds, and because for years it was a case of "any color as long as it's white" . . . well, alyssum was not exactly despised but simply sidelined; it was not considered a serious plant.

This attitude also seemed to infiltrate the seed companies. Although maintaining high quality standards for other seeds, somehow it seemed less critical with alyssum. So, for example, 'Carpet of Snow' produced a carpet that looked as if every cat in the street was asleep underneath.

In recent years, plant breeders have worked hard to change the situation. Plant habit is more predictable and, in particular, there are now many exciting new colors. The seed companies have responded not only by promoting alyssum but also by ensuring that the seed in their packets gives good quality plants.

Until the 1920s alyssum was white. Now there are also cream, various pinks, shades of mauve, apricot, red, deep purple, lemon, and some very pretty bicolors in which the flowers in the center of the spike open one shade and then age to another.

Alyssum is an unusual case in which the mixtures, especially those like 'Aphrodite' and 'Easter Bonnet' with the widest possible range of colors, can be very effective. But not if grown in traditional ways. Sowing the seed direct and thinning to 4–6 in./10–15 cm. gives results that are too unpredictable. Sowing indoors, pricking out, then planting out individually at 6 in./15 cm. creates a jarring series of color blocks.

The way to create a really pretty tapestry of intermingling shades is to sow indoors in cool conditions in individual seed cells. Sow four or five seeds from the mixture in each cell and leave them unthinned. Plant them out without breaking up the individual cells of

potting mix. The individual plants, in their separate colors, will knit together and spread out, and as they come into flower all the colors will meld and be more evenly distributed over the whole planting.

Among all the new colors, the best are the purples like 'Violet Queen', which is both surprising and effective sneaking out across paving from under blue-leaved hostas, and 'Creamery', which looks perfect under and in front of 'Coral Reef' annual phlox in similar tones. This, and newer richer tones also look just right creeping out from under golden hostas. Of the pinks, 'Easter Bonnet Rose' is good in containers with geraniums. I've found the apricot shades rather weak and the red such a strange shade that it seems to fit well with nothing else except other alyssum.

All alyssum, I should say, has some degree of scent but 'Sweet White' is the best, giving a lovely sweet honey fragrance even in partial shade.

Having tried to show that alyssum should be taken a great deal more seriously than its reputation might suggest, I must confess that it can be disappointing. In hot conditions it suffers from powdery mildew and flea beetle and its flowering period can be cut short. Rich soil and plenty of water ensures a longer display but also a slightly more open habit. In cool, moist conditions with no shortage of nutrients in the soil sweet alyssum will often come back quickly after trimming, but in poor, hot, dry conditions you will be left with toasted twigs.

Allowing the plants to self-sow, while initially seeming an attractive and easy option (it runs wild, particularly in parts of the West), is sometimes a mistake. Over the years the clear colors of the more unusual shades are soon watered down and the habit of the plants becomes more and more straggly.

RIGHT *In a little shade, white alyssum is less likely to suffer from the powdery mildew which can be so troublesome in full sun. Here, under old espalier pears, these self-sown plants derive from a mixture sown long ago and have mostly reverted to white. The occasional mauve-flowered plant, the blue lithodora and the ranunculus add highlights and rhythm.*

LEFT *An old favorite and a relative newcomer. 'Carpet of Snow' is a long-established alyssum, although it makes less of a flat carpet than some more modern varieties. Nemophila 'Pennie Black' (correctly N. menziesii subsp. discoidalis) is an intriguing little annual closely related to the more familiar baby blue eyes (N. menziesii). It dislikes dry conditions and is rather fragile so can be damaged in exposed, windy gardens but its deep purple-black flowers edged in white are perfectly partnered here, as they intermingle with the white alyssum.*

Lunaria *Honesty*

Honesty, or money plant, is one of those plants which is always appreciated, but rarely used to its full potential. True, it is valued as a dried flower – for its silvery seedheads that look like coins – and for the wild garden, especially in its delightful but underused white form. But as a spring bedding plant, honesty tends to be ignored. Perhaps because gardeners are locked into the preconception that spring bedders should be a great deal shorter than honesty's 2½ ft./75 cm.

In naturalistic or woodland situations some seedlings are best left where they sow themselves. In any shady situation planted with less delicate woodlanders they can be allowed to do their own thing.

For planting in bedding schemes, raise honesty in pots in the same way as foxgloves (see page 80), but plant out from smaller containers. Honesty plants have relatively sparse root systems and there's even more possibility that soil will fall off the roots than with foxgloves. Space the containers well to encourage the plants to develop a full crown. These will throw more flowers than plants which have been crowded together in their youth.

The purple honesty looks excellent with 'White Triumphator' or yellow 'West Point' tulips or with divisions of the rich pink perennial *Silene dioica* 'Minikin' – this makes a powerful combination, while the white finds a perfect companion in the sultry 'Queen of Night' tulip.

But there are two varieties that will deceive you: variegated forms, spectacularly anemic and gross, which, when their seedlings first appear, are as green as their unvariegated relations. But they break out in blotches – irregular creamy splatts – perhaps I should just mention pigeons . . . 'Variegata' and 'Alba Variegata' are the names to avoid.

Honesty does have a problem or, more accurately, a plague: mosaic virus. The usual symptom is white streaks in the purple honesty flowers. It also attacks wallflowers, brassica crops such as turnips; cabbages and sprouts can also be badly affected. A few misguided gardeners admire the streaky effect but do not be tempted by it; burn the plants at the first sign. Burn any infected wallflowers as well.

LEFT *Testimony that self-sown seedlings can place themselves perfectly among perennial plants. The pure white comfrey,* Symphytum orientale, *is fronted by Spanish bluebells,* Hyacinthoides hispanica, *while behind, in front, and weaving through are the purple flowers of honesty,* Lunaria annua. *Of course the gardener can take a hand in the look of this planting by removing self-sown seedlings from inappropriate positions and moving them to more advantageous ones.*

Matthiola *Stock*

Desirable though they may be as cut flowers, stocks remain deeply unfashionable as garden plants and petulant in hot weather. Nevertheless, there are glints of light in the world of stocks which should set the sensibilities of gardeners stirring. Let's just forget about all those stocks with bewildering names: Trysomic, East Lothian, Selectable Column. They're either fiddly to grow, difficult to overwinter, or discreditably fleeting in flower. There are, however, others which deserve attention.

One is not actually a *Matthiola* but a *Malcomia, M. maritima* (Virginia stock), to be precise. Available only as mixture, the esteem in which it is generally held is indicated by the usual varietal name: 'Mixed'. This is a plant whose status has long been low but sow it in cracks in paving or in gravel, choose the shade you like best from the mix which appears, and each year pull out all the rest until you have an effective stand in just one color.

The wild Mediterranean species, though, are in a class of their own. The splendid *Matthiola tricuspidata* makes a rounded shrub of grayish leaves with spikes of heavily fragrant, rich pink flowers; it's excellent in dry plantings where it self-sows and it makes an arresting combination with *Lathyrus chloranthus* scrambling around – but seed is hard to find.

The night-scented stock, *Matthiola bicornis*, is usually consigned to empty spaces behind taller plants because although the penetrating scent is intoxicating, the flowers (which have always been rather dowdy) only open at night. Even so, it's indispensable, but now there's 'Starlight Sensation' with bolder, brighter colors; it was a top-seller in its first season.

Finally, while most breeders have concentrated on short double-flowered stocks, from Holland come stocks intended to have single flowers. Ridiculed by professional growers, their colors and scents may yet cause a revival of interest. Some catalogs have tried to persuade us that their dumpy double stocks like 'Cinderella' are good for bedding outside. Sadly, this is not the case, although in pots 'Cinderella' can be charming.

Rarely is it suggested that cut-flower stocks such as 'Goldcut', 'Anthony', 'Cleopatra', or 'Sentinel' (which occasionally turn up in catalogs) are used in borders, but in my experiment with 'Sentinel', I found they were very effective. I'll be trying them again.

Matthiola bicornis

OVERLEAF *This peachy single-flowered annual stock, 'Apricot', here mingles with the slightly rosier spikes of* Linaria purpurea *'Canon Went' and the dark-eyed* Potentilla x hopwoodiana *in the pink section of that magical border at Hadspen House in Somerset, England. Even paler, the rarely seen* Collomia grandiflora *sneaks into the picture with lime-green flowering tobacco.*

Mimulus Monkey Flower

And to think that some people have never even grown them . . . they don't know what they're missing! But the virtues of the mimulus are not the usual ones of elegance and a long season. The plants themselves are not especially refined and their season can be short, especially if grown in unsuitable conditions. No, mimulus have other qualities.

Firstly, modern dwarf mimulus can flower in as little as six weeks from sowing. This makes them invaluable plants with which to remedy any mistakes, perfect when you see a gap looming in the border or empty space in a forgotten container, or for a flying start in an early spring as they are unusually hardy too.

All this is fine . . . but if the flowers themselves were uninteresting such virtue would be worthless. Yet the flowers are delightful.

The most widely available Magic Series boasts twelve different plain-faced colors, a few slightly spotted, the colors blending with each other harmoniously. The colors have great subtlety (although you could argue that is like saying some of the colors are a little too similar!). Unfortunately, the absence of the separate colors from most lists means that plants from 'Magic Mixed' or 'Magic Pastel Mixed' must be pricked out individually into 3 in./7 cm. pots, and then you should select the individual colors as

they come into flower. The slightly taller, slightly larger-flowered 'Calypso' comes only as a mixture, but the flowers are powerfully dusted with spots in contrasting colors; 'Viva' comes in just the one shocking color . . . bright yellow with the boldest of mahogany blotches. Wow!

And there's more: mimulus enjoy damp and shady conditions which most annuals do not. In containers on shady patios in town gardens, they're invaluable. True, the converse of this is that in hot and dry seasons they shrivel and die but who cares? We have plenty of other annuals for such situations. Mimulus make splendid companions for other damp-loving plants such as smaller hostas in yellow or with cream or yellow variegations. Choose from the seven colors in the off-white to deep yellow range, some which have contrasting throats or speckles.

And there's another virtue to these native American but British-bred annuals: they make wonderful plantings on their own, either as a mixture or in single colors. Now I can't quite pin down why this is, but it's true.

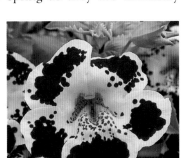

Mimulus *'Viva'*

Mimulus *'Magic Peach'*

Mimulus *'Calypso Mixed' (one color)*

Myosotis *Forget-me-not*

Forget-me-nots – there's no getting away from it – are blue. While pink and white forms are available, it's the blues which retain that clear-eyed glint, that sharp sparkle, which so enlivens the spring garden but which is never gross or overdominant. The pinks, sad to say, are usually a little murky in color and the whites, especially the dwarf forms, age disgracefully,.

There are two other factors to take into account: size and habit. The name 'Blue Ball' says it all; its short, congested, rounded form lacks elegance so I recommend you go for taller varieties. While for tiny spaces a modest habit may be useful, the general demeanor of myosotis is so restrained that they're never overpowering. The name 'Royal Blue' tells you its color, a little overoptimistically, but not that it can reach 16 in./40 cm. in good soil. This is an ideal size both for associating with tulips (most of their long stems are hidden) and for intermingling in more permanent woodland plantings.

In large containers, interplanting with yellow 'West Point' lily-flowered tulips creates an uplifting combination – but, please, not by the bedful as is sometimes still seen in parks. In a large spring planting, break up the border by associating myosotis with wallflowers, polyanthus primroses, and other spring biennials, and use tulips to overlap the individual groups. 'West Point' tulips could straddle the boundary between 'Royal Blue' myosotis and 'Primrose Dame' wallflowers; another lily-flowered tulip like 'White Triumphator' could be set alongside 'West Point' in the forget-me-nots and run into 'Blood Red' wallflowers alongside.

The oddly named 'Blue Basket' and also 'Blue Spire' are shorter at about 12 in./30 cm. and a little less rich in color. 'Victoria Blue' is a little more dwarf still at about 10 in./25 cm., as is the unusually large-flowered 'Music'; all need tulips just a little taller so the tulip flowers are held above the blue foam.

There are, however, situations where the shorter varieties are welcome, which is a relief as the taller types are more difficult to find in catalogs. In semi-shaded woodland plantings, where forget-me-nots are slipped in among hardy geraniums, tiarellas, and woodland phlox, they will stretch out more than they do out in the open sun and lose their congested habit. Even so, 'Blue Ball' will never develop the more relaxed airiness of 'Royal Blue'.

You may be tempted by the other colors: of the pinks,

LEFT *The nodding pure white flowers of* Symphytum orientale *are here accompanied by the intense blue of 'Royal Blue' forget-me-nots, self-sown among the comfrey from the previous year. Allowing forget-me-nots to naturalize often turns up happy associations like this, but over successive generations the flowers may decrease in size and mildew become more prevalent.*

'Rosylva' at 8 in./20 cm., with flowers in a clearer rose pink than most, is certainly the pick; the myosotis listed simply as 'White' is, at 12 in./30 cm., taller than other white forms.

It has been traditional to sow forget-me-nots outside in short rows, then thin and transplant them to their final homes. But seed of some of the newer varieties like 'Rosylva' is relatively expensive, so you may not find much in the packet. Sow it in pots outside or in a cool, well-ventilated greenhouse in summer and prick out into 3 in./7 cm. pots or into trays.

Powdery mildew is the one disfigurement which will be obvious and it can severely limit growth and reduce flowering. It can be especially troublesome in hot springs and as summer approaches, when conditions are naturally encouraging. The taller, more open varieties are less susceptible owing to the better airflow through their more widely spaced shoots. But in some seaons 'Blue Ball' becomes 'Gray Ball'.

LEFT *Myosotis 'Blue Basket', named, I suspect, for its value as a cut flower, creates a sky blue foam through which 'White Triumphator' tulips emerge. Behind, the white is repeated in the flowers of 'Alba Variegata' honesty in a taller, informal style of spring bedding.*

BELOW *The loose airy sprays of* Myosotis *'Royal Blue' intermingle prettily with* Geranium asphodeloides *and gently tone down the intensity of the geranium flowers. Both thrive in the same dappled shade.*

Nemesia *Nemesia*

Nemesias are on a roll; plants go though cycles of fashions and nemesias – at least, where you can grow them – are definitely on the up. And don't they deserve it, for they rival pansies in their range of colors and combinations and in both the glints and softness of their bright and pastel colorings.

The first hint of a revival was the reappearance of some Victorian varieties. True, their history was masked by the seed companies christening them with new names, but revivals they certainly were.

This was the case with the dainty red-and white bicolored variety first known as 'National Ensign', then, when gaining a Royal Horticultural Society Award of Merit in the 1950s, 'Aurora'. It reappeared as 'Mello', and then 'Mello Red & White' as well as 'Danish Flag'. Its blue-and-white counterpart, now almost universally known as 'KLM', was originally 'Twilight'. Just to add to the confusion, these are sometimes listed as 'Miniature Red and White' and 'Miniature Blue and White'. At least the white-eyed 'Blue Gem' kept its original name.

At the same time, some of the old larger-flowered forms in single colors like the self-explanatory 'Fire King' and 'Orange Prince' reappeared along with the 'Tapestry' pastel mixture from which individual shades are now being selected. Indeed, one look at a planting of the 'Tapestry' or 'Carnival' mixtures shows how many gorgeous colors and bicolors are there to be pulled out and developed as separate shades. For nemesias cover as wide a spectrum as any annuals, and with bicolors too there's enormous potential for the development of invaluable shades and combinations.

The problem with nemesias has always been that they're unable to thrive in hot or dry zones and they tend to have a short flowering season. But this makes them especially useful in cooler, damper zones where they not only come into flower quickly but last well. They're also valuable as early starters, planned so that latecomers will spread out into their spaces as they fade away; or as fall-winter extenders in mild areas.

'Sundrops', in a mix of five groups of shades which between them will yield plants in at least twenty different colors, attempts to resolve these problems. Over twenty years in development, this is a very short-growing mixture which when it first flowers does so with an unusual, not-very-nemesia-like flat-topped habit. It then stretches a little, especially in rich conditions. My delight at its long season is tempered by disappointment in its initially inelegant habit.

'KLM', however, is a lovely partner for *Nemophila menziesii* especially as both enjoy the same cool conditions, and their growth habits complement each other so well. 'National Ensign' is more difficult to place, but with 'Multibloom Scarlet Eye' geraniums and *Salvia* 'Fire and Ice', it creates a bold and sparkling show. Blend it with 'KLM' among *Salvia farinacea* 'Strata' and *Begonia* 'Pin-up' to give a new meaning to red, white and blue. In a softer, more intriging style try it with *Viola* 'Bowles Black'.

Gardeners in areas which are too hot for these nemesias to thrive should consider growing *N. foetans* 'Pallida'. Apparently more delicate in constitution, the fine twiggy growth actually stands up better to sun and heat – thanks to its South African origins.

Nemesia *'Blue Gem'*

Nemesia *'Orange Prince'*

LEFT *At first sight this container looks as if color planning has never even crossed the gardener's mind; not so. Some of the plants in this container are there for the long haul, for the all-season display for which so many container plants are valued. Others, in particular the nemesias, are short-term expedients. The conscious thought has been to both create a connection with the color of the yellow evergreen hedge behind and to maintain an inner harmony. The orange nemesia makes the hedge connection boldly from the day it's planted. In the longer term, the bidens will do the job. That orange is a little strident with the rose-pink geranium and phlox, but the white nemesia holds everything together, connecting with the white* Chrysanthemum paludosum *on the other side of the container.*

Nicotiana *Flowering Tobacco*

Gardeners who grow tobacco plants fall into two groups. A sad few are determined to ruin their health at the least possible expense and for them the seed of smoking tobacco, *N. tabacum,* is still available. The rest of us, intent on enjoying our gardens into old age, grow only the ornamental nicotianas and these represent a rare example in which the plant breeders' enthusiasm for reducing the height of their new varieties has actually led to a more versatile plant.

For many years the tall and swaying 'Sensation' and 'Evening Fragrance' types were the standard flowering tobaccos. Reaching 3 ft./90 cm. or more in height, they tend to close their flowers by day, the petals relaxing to limpness, coming alive to release their exotic scent only in the evening. They can be spectacular: given space they develop an attractive rounded, rather airy habit, and their colors show a strange luminosity in evening light. Sadly, they're available only in the unpredictable mixtures rarely required in the borders of color-conscious gardeners.

It is true that the blend of shades is less offensive than in many mixtures – the soft reds and purples, the pinks, mauves and whites harmonize rather than clash in a mass planting. But for planned associations sow early and move the individual seedlings progressively into 5 in./12 cm. pots. Then, by planting time in late spring, the first flowers should be open and each plant can be given a place with the appropriate neighbors.

Nicotiana *Sensation Group*

Nicotiana *'Domino Salmon Pink'*

Among the plants in these mixtures, look out in particular for the rather uncommon white-flowered type, where the backs of the petals are stained red. At the edges, where the petal tissue is at its least substantial, the red shows through to give a striking picotee effect.

Two valuable single colors, the pure white and the lime green, have long had their fanciers. White comes in the form of *N. alata,* also known as *N. affinis,* an elegant plant with height, size of foliage and flowers, degree of branching, and quantity of flowers open at any one time, all in scale. Although reaching 2½–3 ft./75–90 cm. in height, it has foliage which is sufficiently discreet to allow it to be grown in large containers. Its pure white flowers are bold enough to make a visual impact and it has a scent to add its own intoxication to a relaxing drink on a summer's evening. Placing a clump in the sunny angle of a hedge in a city garden ensures that the flowers are set off well and the scent held in the evening air.

Nicotianas have always been known for their unique green shade. This probably derives from decades of selection following a cross made between *N. alata* and the green-flowered *N. knightiana,* itself now available again. Here the modern F_1 hybrid types have let us down. 'Domino Lime' and 'Havana Lime' are a thin and watery shade, quite without passion. They are the result of a further cross involving a white parent and so the rich green is diluted. Most of the old open-pollinated types are stronger in

color but even these vary, so search out, please, the shimmery, more truly lime green found in 'Lime Green' from Unwin's Seeds in England. Its depth of color is outstanding.

The development of F_1 hybrid nicotianas has enabled their height to be reduced and the best (such as the 12–15 in./30–40 cm. Domino Series) have sacrificed little of their natural elegance. But with low plants we tend to look on the flowers from above, rather than view them from the side. The breeders have dealt with this by creating individual flowers whose flat faces are angled upwards so that we see the most color as we look down. Very neat. The flowers also stay open all day but the scent, sad to say, is much lessened.

In the Merlin and Havana series the height has been further reduced – and here the elegance is lost. The resulting plants are too squat for almost anything except display as individual plants in containers. There is, however, temptation in some of the colors: I especially like the warm peachy-pink 'Merlin Peach'.

There are three purple and white bicolors in the Domino Series: 'Domino Picotee' has the largest white center; 'Domino Purple' has a small white center; while 'Domino Purple Bicolor' falls in between. The flowers can provide a link to white plants, the stiff spikes of *Salvia farinacea* 'Cirrus' or the silver foliage of *Helichrysum petiolare*, for example, and are useful where a change in scale is needed after the larger nicotiana foliage and flat-faced flowers. 'Havana Appleblossom', a unique white with

pink backs to the petals, also has a certain charm, despite being sadly dumpy with floppy, untidy flowers.

The soft yet vivid coloring of 'Domino Salmon Pink' looks charming among the small silver leaves of *Plecostachys serpyllifolia*. For a bolder look, it gleams in front of purple *Cotinus coggygria* 'Royal Red' or behind the new American dark-leaved heucheras such as 'Stormy Seas', yet is never garish.

But two unaltered wild species remain the most useful and effective of the whole group, especially in mixed borders. The dainty, waisted green bells of *N. langsdorffii* on their slender wiry stems are spectacular in a fluttery, airy mass. In milder areas this nicotiana often behaves as a good perennial and makes a dense stand of shoots in its second year. This too is wonderful in front of the sultry purple cotinus, although those with a more harmonious turn of mind might find a combination with the smoky pink flowers of *Cotinus coggygria* Purpureus Group more tasteful.

Altogether more majestic is *N. sylvestris*. This is occasionally diminished by a strangely appealing varietal name, 'Only the

LEFT *Tall and swaying* Nicotiana sylvestris, *discreetly supported, shines out against the shrubby background in this mixed border. In front, pink verbenas, 'Black Prince' snapdragons,* Salvia verticillata *'Purple Rain' with its flowers resembling mauve millet, and* Heuchera *'Palace Purple' pick up the color of the purple-leaved cotinus in the background.*

RIGHT *White flowers set against fresh and healthy green foliage always make an impact, without the garishness of bolder contrasts. This planting is themed around the 'Iceberg' Floribunda rose, matching it with* Nicotiana alata, *which grows through, falling forward into the soft and spreading fragrant foliage of 'Chocolate Peppermint' scented geranium. In the following summer, an entirely different grouping in the same colors could complement the rose.*

Nicotiana langsdorffii

Nicotiana tabacum

Lonely'. The great, soft, rather sticky, pale green foliage is impressive from early on but its vital supporting midrib can be damaged in strong winds and then the leaf flops. Give it shelter. (Aphids also have a habit of nestling among the sticky glands, gaining a little protection from sprays. A systemic insecticide on the upper surface of the leaves will kill them.) Sown late, or kept potbound before planting, each plant will produce a single stem, topped by its compact head, with the exceptionally long-tubed flowers with wavy-edged white faces, hanging down.

This is a handsome plant, again a perennial in mild areas, and a fine back-of-the-border spectacle best seen against a sim-

ple and unfussy background such as a hedge or a dark wall (which will also provide the necessary shelter), or soaring up into a clear blue sky. It is a splendid participant in a subtropical summer scheme; placed alongside a large purple ricinus, the white flowers mingle magnificently with the bold shiny foliage of the castor bean plant. Show off the early leaves by planting late-comers in front: plants that will not interrupt the view of the leaves in early summer, but which will hide their imperfections later on in the season. Cannas, perhaps. And, although the leaves do not strike out away from the plant, allow sufficient space for them to develop without smothering their neighbors.

Nigella *Love-in-a-mist*

The Mediterranean region has been the source of some of our most delightful, easy-to-grow and adaptable annuals – including the invaluable nigellas. That they originate in this area, and a knowledge of their adaptations to the climate, should enlighten us to ways of growing these plants which might not otherwise come to mind. We should also recognize that their companions in the wild, with which nigellas look so captivating, can also be their companions in the garden.

Sadly, when most gardeners plan a dry garden or a Mediterranean garden, annuals are forgotten. Shrubs and bulbs predominate and if annuals self-sow from other parts of the garden they may even be removed. But annuals are such a striking feature of many Mediterranean habitats that we should foster a role for them in gardens, where we need to grow them in the same way they grow naturally.

In the wild, nigellas germinate in the late summer and fall, build up a strong root system in fall and winter, and flower prolifically in spring. As the summer approaches, their extensive root system is better able to sustain the plant in the increasingly high temperatures and low rainfall. In gardens, this approach will also encourage an extended flowering season in dry summers.

Most nigellas are no more or less fussy than other Mediterranean annuals, although some of the less familiar species come from the Aegean islands where the winters are especially mild. But sowing in the autumn and allowing a substantial and very attractive rosette to develop ensures that plants start flowering early, yet have the power to continue for as long as those sown in the spring and which begin flowering later.

Nigellas have three features of interest. Their finely dissected foliage creates a pleasing contrast with broader-leaved or more substantial neighbors like euphorbias, acanthus or irises. The flowers are usually blue in the wild, and clear blue is always a valuable color, although other colors such as white and mulberry have been developed in cultivation; then, when the flowers are over, the fat, inflated seed pods with their surrounding spidery bracts continue their appeal.

Nigella damascena is the species from which most varieties are derived, with 'Miss Jekyll' by far the most popular. "One of the annuals that I think is entirely spoilt by dwarfing is Love-in-a-Mist," wrote

Nigella *'Miss Jekyll'*

LEFT *The low tumbling growth of the 'Raubritter' rose with its delightful rounded flowers falls into* Nigella hispanica, *creating an attractive contrast with both the finely cut foliage and the five-petalled flowers. Overwintered seedlings of the nigella become well established during the fall, winter, and early spring when the rose is without its leaves, then flower in conjunction with the rose.*

the good lady in 1899. A hundred years later she would be horrified by the 8 in./20 cm. 'Dwarf Moody Blue' ("compact and miniature hedge-like" according to one catalog) – as am I. She found her eponymous nigella in an old garden in Kent and picked it out especially for its "double flower of just the right degree, and of an unusually fine color." She begged some seed and grew no other until a darker blue type, known as 'Miss Jekyll, Deep Blue', appeared among the pale blues; this too is still found, along with the equally dark, but usefully taller, 'Oxford Blue', reaching 30 in./75 cm.

'Miss Jekyll Rose' and 'Miss Jekyll White' are still sometimes seen. Both are valuable. The rose is especially pretty among blue-leaved euphorbias such as *E. characias* 'Humpty Dumpty' and the white is lovely with pink cistus, rockrose. The 'Persian Jewels' mixture is perhaps a little shorter at 15 in./ 38 cm. and contains both dark and pastel shades. 'Mulberry Rose' has been picked out from the 'Persian Jewels' for listing separately and is disconcerting in opening almost white and steadily darkening to a warm and sumptuous shade.

In recent years, nigella seedheads have been increasingly prized for drying and *N. orientalis* has been introduced for its especially dark, fat seed pods which follow its small yellow-green flowers; it often appears with the varietal name 'Transformer'. *Nigella hispanica* has also appeared and both of these are best allowed simply to self-sow in gravel among drought-loving shrubs and perennials. None are so overbearing that their neighbors will be smothered and their demure qualities ensure they fit in anywhere.

RIGHT *At Christopher Lloyd's garden at Great Dixter, Sussex, England, permanent and temporary plantings mingle together. The bold magenta spikes of* Gladiolus communis subsp. byzantinus, *taking over from the metallic footballs of* Allium cristophii, *are surrounded by* Nigella 'Oxford Blue' *and the rich, dusty purple foliage of the red orach,* Atriplex hortensis 'Red Plume'. *The orach needs careful attention. It can self-sow too prolifically and smother smaller plants and as it does so its color may vary; remove those plants which are badly placed or which show pale foliage.*

Papaver *Shirley and Opium Poppy*

The red cornfield poppy has a strong pull on our emotions: poppies soaked the battlefields of the World War I as trenches were dug and soil mounded, and so the red poppy has become the symbol of the American Legion. As emblems of those killed, on November 11th – Veteran's Day – both here and in Britain, we again remember. Wherever the British colonized, poppies are usually found, as emigrants took poppies with them – as stowaways in their precious wheat.

Variants of this scarlet Flanders field poppy, *Papaver rhoeas*, must have appeared regularly in the wild before selective weedkillers; occasionally, they still do. But it was not until 1879, when the Reverend Wilks of Shirley in Surrey, southern England, noticed a form with a white edge to the flower in a field adjoining his new garden, that the potential of these annual poppies as garden flowers was first recognized.

From this one plant he developed single- and double-flowered strains in softer colors, and twenty years later he had also eliminated the black blotch at the base of each petal. Then in the middle 1900s, the English painter Cedric Morris selected poppies, retaining particularly those with misty and smoky tints, picoteed flowers, gray tones and subtle whiskering and veining; anything red was banished. These are variously known as 'Angel's Wings', 'Fairy Wings', 'Mother of Pearl', or 'Cedric Morris'.

More recently, 'Angel's Choir', the double-flowered form of 'Fairy Wings', has been developed; although the fuller flowers lack the simple purity of their progenitors, they last a little longer.

Papaver somniferum 'Peony Flowered Mixed' (single color)

Papaver rhoeas 'Shirley Single Mixed' (single color)

In USDA zones seven and south, the simplest way to raise these poppies is to scatter the seeds through mixed borders or along the edges of gravel drives; late summer is the best time. Plants then develop an extensive root system and a spreading rosette of foliage during the warm days of autumn and mild spells in winter. When the days begin to stretch in spring, at about the time for a spring sowing, the plants are already well established and ready to capitalize on longer days and increasing temperatures well ahead of spring-sown poppies. Much larger plants with far more flowers are the result, together with a slightly earlier and noticeably longer flowering season. However, in most zones sowing in spring can also produce good results; prompt thinning and no check to growth enable plants to establish quickly and flower prolifically.

As plants develop from a spring or autumn scattering, you can easily remove those in unsuitable places and leave others to fill out. Any flowering in colors which are out of harmony with neighboring plants can be pulled as their first flowers open. Unless deadheading is faultless, you may then have poppies forever.

RIGHT *Just a few poppies can make a very big difference. In one sense the annual chrysanthemums, Chrysanthemum segetum, dominate this natural blend of spring-sown, British native cornfield annuals. But the few fully open poppy flowers, Papaver rhoeas, and the spattering of soon-to-be open buds are enough to deflect our attention. Cornflowers, Centaurea cyanus, and corn chamomile, Anthemis arvensis, complete the picture.*

From Shakespeare to Keats and beyond, the opium poppy, *Papaver somniferum,* has also gripped our emotions . . . one way or another. Some gardeners are still wary of growing it, believing that the drug squad will drag them off to jail as soon as they're spotted. While local ordinances may vary from place to place, suffice to say that growing *P. somnifernum* strictly as an ornamental will add some valuable and fascinating flowers to your garden flora. Forms of this species have one special additional feature which other annual poppies lack: superb foliage. For this reason it's important to grow them well; in badly grown poppies the substance of the plant and the leaves suffer first.

In most areas, opium poppies are insufficiently hardy for an autumn sowing, but do develop strongly from a spring sowing. From an early stage their glaucous, blue-gray foliage is an attraction; set against the freshness of succulent delphinium shoots, it's a treat.

Garden varieties have diverged from the simple wild single mauve in both color and flower form. There are some astonishing fluffy doubles, usually called peony-flowered, in mixtures, or better still, in single colors like 'Black Peony', a shimmering, rich maroon-purple. There are also frilly-feathered doubles, again in separate colors, such as the gorgeous 'White Cloud'. Even more unexpected is a form with especially large seed pods, a form with especially *small* pods, and even a hen-and-chickens form with tiny seed pods tightly clustered around a single larger pod.

Again, deadheading is vital. Nip the pods off before they drop their seeds, or cut them on long stems to dry, and leave just a pod or two on plants whose flowers you especially like to shed their seed. If the color is crucial, deadhead them all and resow bought seed the following spring.

ABOVE LEFT Papaver somniferum.

LEFT Poppies and climbing roses may seem an unlikely combination but here the simple but enticing flowers of a self-sown opium poppy are carried on tall-enough stems to reach in among the flowers of Rosa 'Compassion' as it scrambles around the window. A few snaking twirls of jasmine and clematis foliage feature in the background.

Pelargonium Geranium

You have to be so careful with geraniums. Gardeners roll them out in scarlet sheets to emblazen Disney World, and in town and city plantings all over the world they dazzle residents and visitors alike. And they sure are bright.

For the summer bedding display outside Buckingham Palace in London they even match the color of their red geraniums with that of the traditional guardsmen's jackets. But those vast beds . . . full of geraniums . . . lined up in rows . . . should gardening simply be about color that hits you between the eyes and leaves you senseless? Fortunately, there are other ways.

I plant scarlet geraniums and so should you . . . the important question is: how? Nowhere should they be planted in such unrelenting red. And that old red-white-and-blue style, with the alyssum and the lobelia: that's out too.

Of course, there's nothing intrinsically wrong with red – far from it. And if you look at the wonderful range of seed-raised geraniums now available, you can have any shade of red you like; there are plenty, and any shade of pink too, and cerise and orange and purple and white with an increasing range of bicolors.

So within an admittedly limited spectrum there's a valuable range of shades from which to choose and also an increasing range of styles: the habit of growth and the type of flower head varies greatly. Some are close to traditional cuttings-raised geraniums with big, bold heads; this was the aim of plant breeders when they developed 'Nittany Lion', the first F_1 hybrid geranium back in the 1960s. Some modern series incorporate genetic material from wild species to create varieties like those in the Sensation Series with more florets, but less crowded petals.

Frankly it's all too complicated to set out in detail without filling half the book. So let me summarize by use. For a traditional scarlet geranium to grow with 'Limelight' licorice plant, or with bronze beet and sparks of bidens, or with silver cinerarias, go for 'Horizon Deep Scarlet' with its impressive leaf zoning; 'Maverick Scarlet' is a chunkier alternative.

In a more informal arrangement, with daintier companions like the sinuous trails of *Plecostachys serpyllifolia* or that new favorite *Lobelia* 'Regatta Blue Splash', *Pelargonium* 'Sensation Scarlet' is superb. 'Sensation Picotee', in white with a red rim and red speckles, is the most gorgeous geranium yet created and would also fit. Even grown in a container on its own 'Sensation Picotee' is simply captivating.

LEFT *Breeders have given up developing yellow- and pink- leaved geraniums, it's simply not possible genetically. Now they've adopted a different approach to foliage color, and this soon-to-be-released variety boasts an unusually large dark zone on the leaf with a narrow green edging. Here, it grows with nasturtium foliage and the cuttings-raised* Verbena *'Pastel Pink'.*

The Sensations produce more flower heads than any other variety available and they're almost never attacked by botrytis; the fading petals drop off rather than stay in place to rot.

For bedding in a traditional style, the Avanti and Multibloom series are best in a large expanse where they'll get little special treatment. There are bold colors and more subtle and unusual shades in both series. 'Multibloom Lavender', for example, is a soft yet strong lavender-pink shade and perfect for the pastel combinations that we all still secretly love; try it with silver foliage, with the pink daisies of *Brachyscome* 'Strawberry Mousse', or with 'Floral Showers Lavender' snapdragon. 'Avanti Apricot Bicolor', also known as 'Rosy Sunset', is orange with a hint of pink and a white eye and is stunning with purple perilla, with the picotee *Impatiens* 'Tempo Peach Frost' peeping out from underneath, or with those bronze beetroot leaves about which I'm always enthusing. On a smaller scale, in good soil, the Sensations are impossible to beat.

Another for this multi-mixed intermingling style, and for ground cover, is the superb Tornado Series of ivy-leaved geraniums with their almost flat habit of growth and flower heads in carmine, lilac-pink, or white, standing up from the foliage. 'Breakaway Red', a denser ground cover geranium incorporating blood from wild species, is unjustly overlooked.

For containers, especially the jostling plantings which are so much more interesting than those in the old-fashioned blockier style, you'll find that in the moist, rich conditions which prevail when containers are well looked after, most geraniums develop a taller, slightly more open habit than they do in the open ground. The result is a plant which may spread out a little more, but which also smothers its neighbors less pugnaciously. So any plants like trailing lobelia, strawflowers, plecostachys, bushy convolvulus,

LEFT *Red geraniums can find a home anywhere, even at a prestigious garden like Hidcote Manor, Gloucestershire, England, but they need the right companions. Here, in a wooden container set against blue painted boarding, they're interplanted with* Helichrysum petiolare *'Limelight', the long stiff stems emerging among the foliage and flowers of the geranium to create a bright but not uncomfortably flashy association.*

bidens, petunias, and even violas and pansies – any with a tendency to develop slender stems – will penetrate the geranium foliage and peep through to create interesting associations.

Before discussing how to raise them, perhaps it's worth selecting a few special varieties from the many series available: 'Horizon Deep Scarlet' (deep red, well zoned); 'Multibloom White' (best all-round white); 'Raspberry Ripple' (red and white stripes); 'Sensation Picotee' (unique white with red edge and specks); 'Tango Orange' (best orange); 'Tornado White/Pink' (white ivy-leaved for ground cover); 'Maverick Star' (white with pink eye); and 'Vogue Appleblossom' (soft appleblossom pink).

Geraniums are not the easiest of plants to raise from seed, although modern seed technology has ensured that they're a great deal less difficult than they once were. The seed is expensive, so now that the seed is pre-prepared to make germination speedier and more even, it represents somewhat better value than in the past.

Space sow the seeds in late winter or early spring in a 3 in./ 7 cm. pot of moist, peat-based potting mix, cover with their own depth of sifted mix, cover the pot with plastic wrap, and place in the dark at a temperature of 70°F/21°C. Move them into the light (but not the sun) as soon as they germinate, usually in about ten days. When they've developed their first true leaves, move the seedlings into individual 2½ in./6 cm or 3 in./7 cm. pots to grow on. There's no need to pinch them, but try to allow enough space on the greenhouse bench to encourage branching.

When planting out, geraniums in particular seem to benefit from watering in with a liquid fertilizer, and I find it also pays to pick off any flowers and buds. Then they romp away.

RIGHT *This densely planted red bed contains no more than three plants of any one variety – and sometimes only a single plant. 'Breakaway Red' geranium is being invaded by 'Hermine Grashoff' nasturtiums which will need to be controlled. Dahlia 'Scarlet Emperor' is just about to start to flower while to its right Amaranthus 'Hopi Red Dye' is reaching its peak. Salvia coccinea 'Lady in Red' peeps out all over the place and, in front of the wild white petunias, 'Rambo', the tallest and bushiest of all the Salvia splendens varieties, is filling out well.*

Petunia **Petunia**

The petunia embraces every current trend in the development of annuals and bedding plants. While some annuals are popular for borders and some for containers, petunias are spectacular in both. Breeders are fixated upon producing ever more dwarf varieties of some annuals – and vigorous, trailing varieties of others; petunias are developing in both directions. Reviving old varieties is popular in some annuals, while new introductions fuel interest in others; in petunias it's both.

Gardeners and garden centers, seed companies and plant breeders are taking an interest in all types of petunia, using a wide yet still increasing range of varieties in both traditional and newly creative ways. So there's a great deal to say about petunias in a relatively small space.

Petunias are nothing if not colorful. And with breeders developing so many (one trade catalog lists 162 different varieties – not including mixtures; this parallels the China asters of a century ago), the fine variations of color and the huge range of color combinations allow the most precise selection for carefully color-themed plantings. Petunias sparkle; they are vibrant, and quintessentially summery, stunning in dry summers and more colorful than many annuals in dull ones; some types are even scented.

The most recent trend looks to the past. Two wild species, both of them quite early participants in petunia development, have emerged from botanic gardens and into seed catalogs and garden centers. _Petunia axillaris_, its white flowers delicately patterned with speckled streaks the color of Dijon mustard, has proved a vigorous and surprisingly weather-resistant plant. Its relaxed, open habit endears it to those of us frustrated at the impossibility of using the many more compact petunias in informal mixed border plantings.

And _P. integrifolia_, in bold magenta-purple, with its more spreading habit, has been used in the breeding of some of the cuttings-raised hanging basket varieties like the Surfinias. This too is a good border petunia, without the intense branching and discordant density of color which would disrupt plantings of perennials and old-fashioned annuals.

At the other extreme is the still-evolving Fantasy (or Fantasia) Series, sometimes known as the Junior Petunia. Small, flat or slightly rounded plants, their flowers are also unusually small, and the whole plant rather stiff in its bearing. Although so weak as to be useless in beds and borders unless fed and watered almost daily, in containers, and especially when unfettered by competition, this can be a very pretty plant; a blend of harmonizing shades looks delightful in a terra-cotta strawberry pot.

By contrast, seed-raised trailing varieties to match the cuttings-raised Surfinias are also benefiting from

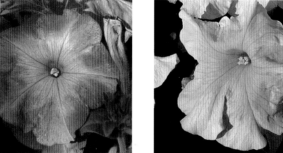

Petunia _'Horizon Lavender Sunrise'_

Petunia _'Prism Sunshine'_

Petunia _'Fantasy Pink Morn'_

LEFT *Unlikely companions: two matching colors from the Petunia 'Plum Crazy' mixture fill in cleverly around the bare leaf stems of* Geranium palmatum, *which, where necessary, can be wheeled under cover in late autumn for extra winter protection. The 'Florence White' bachelor's button is probably an unnecessary addition. Around the tub, the billowing green flowers of lady's mantle, Alchemilla mollis, make a soft frame. When they fade, and the masterwort astrantias in the background are cut down, the petunia will have developed sufficiently to capture the attention regardless of its surroundings. A stray yellow petunia from the mix has been set to the side to blend with the alchemilla.*

determined attention and proving unexpectedly adaptable. Frankly, these petunias are less than elegant falling in curtains from baskets. They are, though, undeniably colorful, and grown in the garden as ground cover they can be both arresting and stylish; those in the Wave Series hold their flowers up more dependably than the cuttings-raised types. Even the almost-lurid 'Purple Wave' will make you gasp – with delight, as clumps of

late-summer colchicums surge through. 'Misty Lilac', in softest lilac-pink, is a cool background for white colchicums or can be planted through an enriching spring mulch to snake out enticingly from under or up into roses.

In cool damp summers or very humid ones the weather can ruin petunias; somewhere, during the journey from wild species to F_1 hybrid bedding plant, intolerance of bad weather had been allowed to become almost endemic, especially in the larger-flowered Grandiflora types. (This may well have been because the breeders work almost entirely in areas with warm, sunny summer climates.) The smaller-flowered Multifloras have always shown more tolerance and better recovery, and in both groups the rich rose is the most weather-resistant color, with dark red showing particular susceptibility. Now that weather resistance has become a priority, the Storm Series is one of the best for tolerating wet weather and recovering afterwards.

But it is color that drives so much development, and new colors are now both tempting and bewildering gardeners. 'Prism Sunshine' marked a big step forward in yellow petunias, as much in seed quality as in color, productivity, and reliability. In the garden this is splendid with 'Pagoda' parsley, curly kale 'Redbor' or 'Zenith Red' Afro-French marigolds.

'Horizon Lavender Sunrise' is the most dramatic of the newer yellow-throated varieties which are almost impossible to use in the garden – except on their own or, in the case of this petunia, with a variety of the licorice plant, *Helichrysum petiolare* 'Limelight'; paler shades with paler throats are more accommodating to other nearby colors. Pale yellow- or cream-centered Morn types are a recent development; the cool and captivating 'Celebrity Chiffon Morn', so prolific as well as being almost ethereal in its coloring, combines perfectly with the silver foliage

LEFT *The airy growth and wiry stems of* Gaura lindheimeri *look their best against a more rounded background, and the eye goes straight to them. When the occasional flower of* Petunia *'Pearl Rose & White' sparks through from behind, it adds a third dimension to an intimate planting. The small-flowered, but prolific Pearl Series is again finding favor in reaction to the bigger, brighter, and blowsier types.*

of licorice plants or cineraria, with palest watered-blue petunias, and with clean whites.

Veined types, such as the Plum Multifloras and Daddy Grandifloras, are good in small spaces where the two, usually harmonious, colors of background and veining bring adaptability to small spaces. The startling red-on-blushed-white 'Strawberry Sundae' and the six individual shades of the Celebrity Ice Series are the most choice, and provide the opportunity to coordinate neighboring colors with either the background color or the veins. Even a single plant from these series has character.

Doubles always spark interest but are poor in wet climates. The Multiflora Duo Series of semi-doubles combines enough fullness of flower with the best weather resistance to create a viable series; 'Duo Silvery Shades', purple-veined pale lilac, is the pick in character, color, and performance. The Grandiflora Pirouettes are the Dolly Partons of the petunias: bigger, blowsier, and altogether more full. But a downpour ruins the colorful display with no compensating diversions. In porches and conservatories (where the Victorians always grew the doubles) and reliably sunny climates, they truly amaze.

There are so many series, some so very similar, that it might be helpful to narrow down the range. This is my choice:

Grandiflora Double: Pirouette Series
Multiflora Double: Duo Series
Grandiflora Single: Storm Series or Daddy Series (veined)
Multiflora Single: Mirage Series or Celebrity Series
Trailing: Wave Series

RIGHT *Two petunias, both in shades of rose pink, show how carefully selected varieties from entirely different series can look good together. In the background is the taller 'Marshmallow', which fades as the flowers age, and in the foreground, the paler 'Celebrity Chiffon Morn'. In this planting, both provide the background against which to admire the unusual smoky pink of Chinese forget-me-not, Cynoglossum 'Mystery Rose'. The blue is more common but this pink cynoglossum is altogether more subtle yet stands up well against the larger flowers of the petunias. It can be raised as a biennial, though it appreciates good winter drainage, but has here made a well-branched plant in rich soil from a spring sowing.*

But which are scented? Most petunias have a little perfume but few modern varieties are well scented. Go back to the old (and cheap) open-pollinated mixtures and also the F_2 mixtures, mostly in watered-pinks and mauves; there you'll find scent. But not the flower power, the colors, or the dependability of modern varieties; the breeders are working on it.

Phlox Annual Phlox

The popularity of perennial summer garden phlox has been constant for decades and the dependability of the alpine phlox like *P. douglasii*, probably makes them as popular among new gardeners as the perennials. At the same time interest in the smaller woodland phlox like *P. divaricata* has broadened with a growing enthusiasm for shade gardening and the arrival of new introductions. But it's a little bewildering. . . only quite recently, with the introduction of some superb new varieties, have the native Texan annual phlox, *P. drummondii,* again found favor. For, as is the case with so many annuals, phlox have known good times before the recent lean years . . . .

In the late 1880s, England's Suttons Seeds listed 39 varieties, including a double and a semi-double form, plus various mixtures; by the 1920s the total was still a very respectable 28. In the 1980s and early 1990s many catalogs were down to just three or four varieties, and quality deteriorated, hence the red rogue among my 'Blue Beauty' on page 144. Then interest among breeders was revived: new pot plants were the first aim, followed by new doubles and semi-doubles; then taller mixtures, then old varieties such as 'Leopoldii' reappeared.

There are two features which make annual phlox so delightful. First, the color range: the variety of color combinations possible, and now becoming available, is the most diverse of all the annuals except perhaps pansies and violas. Second, the habit of the plants, except the very smallest, is naturally conducive to the style of intimate planting which suits today's gardens. For the plants branch rather strongly, given space, yet the rigidity of the stems and the occasional natural openings which develop allow other plants to intertwine without smothering the phlox.

The smallest varieties are the least suitable for the garden. 'Dolly Mixed' and the double-flowered 'Chanal' are good as autumn-sown pot plants for greenhouses, as they are less inclined to stretch; both are too dumpy in the garden. 'Palona' has a good range of colors and a slightly more relaxed habit, but the look is spoiled by the edges of the petals of some colors curling rather than lying flat.

Moving up in size, 'Cecily' has been revived as 'Cecily Old & New Shades', a lovely blend of colors with some unusual lavenders, pinks, and creams. The expanding Buttons Series comes in bolder colors, is ideal in size and habit and its separate colors are increasingly easy to find, as is its formula mixture of separate colors, 'Buttons Mixed'. 'Buttons Blue Shades' is a rich but cool harmonious blend of purplish blues with pale eyes and is lovely

LEFT *The vivid magenta-tinted red of this single color from the 'Buttons and Bows' mixture of annual phlox mingles intimately with* Anagallis *'Skylover' whose slender, inquisitive stems insinuate themselves among the more rigid stems of the phlox to create a delightful picture.*

RIGHT *Although the dark red is a little tall and the scarlet a little bold, 'Fantasy Mixed' phlox shows an appealing harmony in color tones and a reasonably even height across the colors. There are some especially delightful colors in the mix.*

with *Salvia farinacea* 'Strata' and silver foliage; 'Buttons Cherry White Eye' is bright, clean, and good with dark red geraniums and *Hibiscus acetosella*, with its purple-bronze, maple-like leaves.

Stocks of the old favorite, the taller Beauty Series, are less true than they were and almost unavailable in separate colors, but the cream, when you can find it, is simply gorgeous. Then there are two particularly enticing taller mixtures, 'Coral Reef' and 'Tapestry', at about 14 in./35 cm. 'Coral Reef', also known as 'Phlox of Sheep', comes in a blend of pinks, peach, apricot, and coral shades, and yellows and creams. You can pick from its shades of languidly summery harmony to use individually. 'Tapestry' may be naturally less companionable as a blend but features rare colors and color combinations; here too, you can pick out individuals to make themed groupings. One special feature of the mid-height 'Tapestry' and 'Cecily Old & New

Shades' mixtures is the presence of so many bicolors. This allows bi-colored individuals to be used as transitional plants, linking with other plants in each of the two colors.

The tallest (at 18 in./45 cm.) of those easily available, and a superb cut flower and mid-border variety, is 'Leopoldii', introduced from Texas in 1835 yet still surviving. The rose-pink flowers have a white center and a lovely scent, especially late in the day. We need more colors in this height.

Raising annual phlox is not difficult, although all varieties need space to encourage branching and the smaller ones appreciate regular liquid feeding. Starting them in pots gives them the best chance to develop well; in southern zones, they can be direct-seeded in fall and grown as winter annuals. All benefit from careful deadheading; this is tricky, but the improvement in length of flowering is dramatic.

RIGHT *Evidence that when the best-laid plans go awry, the result may not necessarily be a disaster. Heliotropium 'Marine' dominates the foreground here with the arching branches of the gray-leaved Helichrysum petiolare making an attractive contrast with the metallic flush in the heliotrope foliage. Phlox 'Blue Beauty' emerges behind with Salvia farinacea 'Victoria', but a single rogue red phlox, which came unexpectedly in the 'Blue Beauty', adds a fiery spark among the pimpernel, Anagallis 'Skylover'.*

Primula Polyanthus and Primrose

The primrose of the English countryside may have a romantic appeal for American gardeners but, sadly, this is not matched with an ability to thrive in all American gardens. The English primrose is at its best in shady conditions in the cooler, damper English counties, where the climate is most akin to that of the Pacific Northwest. The polyanthus primrose, which has the additional blood of a species from drier conditions, is noticeably more adaptable and the most popular series worldwide, the Pacific Giants, was actually bred in California. Both are very different from the candelabra primroses and other woodland and waterside perennial primulas.

The polyanthus primroses were developed from the hybrid between the English primrose (*Primula vulgaris*) and the cowslip (*P. veris*). Most F_1 hybrid polyanthus now grown for bedding are vulgar, marred by overlarge flowers which weigh down the stems, especially after spring showers. So many are intentionally bred with garish yellow eyes to the flowers, the better to create a contrast with the basic color, that they're impossible to use except in old-fashioned confetti-colored mixtures or in last-resort combinations with yellow tulips.

The 'improved' primroses sold as pot plants also have their faults: they're weak, the flowers are gross, and the colors are garish. Even the flowers of those in a true primrose color are usually so disproportionately large as to have no place in the garden. But enough – let's turn to the real beauties among the polyanthus.

Fortunately, there was Florence Bellis of Gresham, Oregon, and Major Knocke of

Barnhaven polyanthus Harvest Yellows

Barnhaven polyanthus Cowichan Amethyst Group

Cowichan Station, British Columbia, and to them we owe the fact that this chapter even appears in the book. For without these two, there would be so few beautiful primroses and polyanthus to write about that I would be tempted to leave out this entry.

In 1934 Florence Bellis spent $4.90 of her last $5 on some polyanthus seed from Suttons in England. Her good eye and her innocent enthusiasm led to the selection of her Silver Dollar strains (so-called from the size of the flowers) and the huge range of Barnhaven polyanthus and primroses that we have today.

Then in a Cowichan garden in the early 1930s, Major Knocke spotted a polyanthus which lacked the usual bright yellow eye. It seemed sterile, but the good major split it and passed it around, and ten years later Florence Bellis found some pollen in its flowers. This was the beginning of what is now a five-color series of lustrous polyanthus without garish contrasts.

The Cowichan Group polyanthus come in five groups of shades: Garnet, in garnet, blackish-garnet, and ruby shades; Amethyst, in violet and amethyst blue; Blue, in various rich blues, some with black eyes; Venetian, in strawberry and hot-pink shades; and Yellow, with dark stems and bronzed foliage.

Sadly, the trials of these plants at the Royal Horticultural Society's garden at Wisley in England showed that we may have more florid catalog prose than fine flowers, since all were too variable to be depended upon for carefully planned displays. But among them were a few plants of such poise and such elegant posture, such deep color and such sumptuous richness, such luster, such calm restraint, such prolific flowering, and such harmonious association of flower color, stem color, and leaf tone – well, I've grown them for years, either from bought seed or my own, and they are gorgeous.

As an example, try yellow Cowichans with Bowles' golden grass (*Milium effusum* 'Aureum'), blue forget-me-nots such as 'Light Blue' with its pale flowers and tall open habit, or with blue wood anemones. Plant them too among *Euphorbia donii*, whose red-tinted emerging stems pick up the color in the Cowichans, or under *Daphne* x *houtteana*.

Florence Bellis's original Silver Dollar Series still comes in almost two dozen different colors or shades. Some are clean and pale, some rich and lustrous, some have dark stems and dark leaves, some have a white or blue rim to the petals. Even some of those with a large yellow eye are pretty because the surrounding flower color is so serene.

These and her other strains are all so superior in terms of color that only uniformity recommends the F_1 hybrids; if you must, choose the Pacific Giants, Rainbow, or Crescendo series.

Non-polyanthus primroses have also developed enormously but they're rarely used in spring bedding. Almost all varieties are bred as pot plants and are without the hardiness required to thrive after a wet winter in the open ground. The Barnhaven primroses are an exception, though they come in far fewer shades; many have the dark leaves and dark stems which set off the flowers so well. Most maintain the general habit of the wild primrose but are much more prolific; some of the colors, especially the apricot shades in Osiered Amber Group and the sultry reds of Tartan Red Group, are captivating.

Grow them with species crocus and other dwarf spring bulbs (even in a windowbox), with *Cyclamen coum*, with the fresh fronds of dwarf ferns like the beech fern, *Thelypteris phegopteris*, or with celandines and wood anemones. Wood anemones are increasingly available in the pinks and pale blues which associate well with these primroses, and *Anemone* x *lipsiensis*, the hybrid between *A. nemerosa* and *A. ranunculoides*, with its pale yellow flowers and bronze-tinted foliage, is an ideal companion.

At Barnhaven, they recommend this sowing procedure: sow

ABOVE *This small garden assembly centers on the wild cowslip (*Primula veris*) with blue Cowichan Group polyanthus on either side; they could be the start of some strange hybrids. The yellow-leaved feverfew seedlings will fill the space in summer, along with the foliage from the* Pulmonaria saccharata *in the background and the few slender yellow leaves of Bowles' golden grass (*Milium effusum *'Aureum') which will expand into bolder, but still delicate, clumps.*

the seed in February (March or April in especially cold areas) using seed trays and a peat-based potting mix; do not cover the seed. Water well, then cover the seed tray with an identical overturned tray and place in the shade. Germination should take place, they say, in two to three weeks – uncover them then – and prick out the seedlings when they have at least four true leaves.

Needless to say, I've adapted this system – partly so that half a dozen varieties can be sown in a smaller space than that occupied by six seed trays. Sowing in February is fine. The seed does not require frost to spark germination, so keep the seed in the fridge to prolong its viability before sowing in late winter. Home-saved seed is best sown as soon as possible after collection, in midsummer – as long as you can keep it cool.

I sow in 3½ in./9 cm. pots of equal parts peat-based and soil-based potting mix. The mix is firmed gently and topped with ¼ in./6 mm. of sharp grit; the seed is sown on the grit and watered in carefully. I then place the pots in the cold frame and cover it with something solid to keep out the light – I use an old wooden door. The trick is to keep them shaded and moist; the seeds must not dry out.

Modern F_1 hybrids are more vigorous and can be sown as late as June, but keeping the temperature below the 65°F/18°C at which germination is impeded can be very difficult in summer. After germination, I prick out into 3 in./7 cm. pots, three seedlings in each, then split them and move them on into individual 3½ in./9cm pots later.

Choosing the right time for planting out is not easy. Both primroses and polyanthus need time to establish themselves before the winter, but planting too early, or in excessively rich soil, can promote a mass of soft growth susceptible to disease.

The big pest problem with primroses and polyanthus is root weevil. The adults nibble the edges of the leaves and their ginger-headed white larvae feed on the roots; primulas are their favorite food. Pesticides are ineffective but biological control, in the form of parasitic nematodes, though expensive, often works well on young plants in pots – less so in garden soil.

One of the joys, and drawbacks, of Barnhaven polyanthus and primroses is that most are very variable. When the seedlings flower in their first spring there's an opportunity to select your favorites and retain them for future years, splitting them regularly after flowering. Collecting seed from them, however, will provide unpredictable results. The flowers of all primulas are constructed to prevent self-pollination and facilitate cross-pollination, so the seed from any one plant is unlikely to produce a batch of identical seedlings. Go back to new seed each year.

Barnhaven primrose (single color)

Barnhaven polyanthus Striped Victorian Group (single color)

Ricinus Castor Bean Plant

Big, bold and beautiful effects are enjoying a comeback and with them the castor bean plant. If you have *Fatsia japonica* in the garden many visitors will quickly identify it as the plant that is the source of castor oil – but they'd be wrong. *Ricinus communis*, with its poisonous but gloriously fat and speckled seeds (just opening the packet is a treat), is the true castor bean plant. Since the last century, it has been a vital constituent of the once-fashionable, now reviving, subtropical bedding schemes. Palms and bananas were wheeled out of greenhouses and bedded out for the summer; seed-raised castor bean plants fitted in perfectly.

For the largest and most dramatic castor bean plants – and that, after all, is the point – seeds (which are very poisonous if eaten) should be sown early, a single seed in a 3 in./7 cm. pot at 70°F/20°C. The seedlings should then be moved into increasingly large containers so that when they're planted out from 8 in./20 cm. pots they hit the border running, so to speak, and romp away to produce plants with real impact and a variety of leaf colors and flower shades. By the end of the season the plants could reach 8–9 ft./2.4–2.7 m. high. Plan accordingly.

These large and luxuriant leaves are easily damaged in windy situations. So, use castor bean plants in sheltered places; once the vein along the center of each leaf is broken, the leaf hangs limp. The leaves can also be disfigured simply by rattling against each other.

A whole grove of castor bean plants in their various color forms is an impressive sight. Unfortunately, a harmonious effect is less easy

Ricinus communis

to achieve than it might appear, as catalogs can be unhelpful. What can you do when a variety is listed as 'Mixed', yet described as having leaves in "bright green"? Don't buy it, of course. Fortunately, the leaf colors are usually obvious by planting-out time, and individuals can be selected for precise planting sites at this stage; fortunately again, the heights given in catalogs are usually a little more dependable – allowing for a little exaggeration in the dwarfness of the recently introduced smaller varieties.

The form usually listed as *Ricinus* var. *zanzibarensis* will reach 6 ft./1.8 m. in height and often more in most suitable gardens without special treatment. It usually comes in a mix of dark green, various greens with a silvery-gray sheen, and purplish or bronze shades. 'Gibsonii', a bronze selection, is equally tall. 'Impala', at 4–6 ft./1.2–1.8 m., in deep, shimmering bronze, has been one of the best of all for many years but is disappearing in favor of the similar but even shorter 'Carmencita', with red flowers, and 'Carmencita Pink', both of which have the benefit of flowering dependably.

As well as creating spectacular groves, castor bean plants can be used with other bold or exotic seed-raised plants such as *Nicotiana sylvestris*, cleomes, sunflowers, the tall forms of *Lupinus hartwegii* such as 'Sunrise', *Convolvulus* 'Star of Yelta', and climbing nasturtiums. If they're available, add bananas, palms, and other tender plants which can spend the summer in the garden and boast a similar boldness.

LEFT *Single specimens of castor
bean plant can add quite a punch
to mixed borders. Here, a few
plants of 'Carmencita' have been
slipped in between 'Heritage', one
of David Austin's English roses,
and 'Sonata Mixed' cosmos and
give the whole planting a quirky
and strangely intriging air.*

Rudbeckia *Gloriosa Daisy*

Consider the native American rudbeckias. These are among the most valuable of summer annuals - the perennial black-eyed Susans having long proven themselves - combining good color, long flowering period and robustness. Their quirky style takes them beyond the range of their relations, the French marigolds, and into a class where character has survived the plant breeders' inclination towards miniaturization. Even 'Toto', one of the smallest at about 10 in./25 cm., with flowers in a flat plane at the top of the plant, has retained some individuality (although 'Becky', a mixture with larger flowers on shorter plants, has not).

But, at the same time, rudbeckias will never be as uniform as marigolds. So the consistently double flowers of 'Goldilocks' made it a well-deserved award winner in its time, but now you'll find plants with intensely double flowers mixed with those carrying far fewer petals. 'Kelvedon Glory', reintroduced as 'Sonora', should have single or slightly semi-double flowers with a mahogany blotch on each petal but some may be unblotched.

All this is disconcerting only by contrast with rigid expectations. In my favorite mahogany and yellow plantings, the variation in doubling is only irritating if it reduces impact at a certain point in the border. There may be variation in color too, but in the rough-and-tumble of such plantings this can even be an advantage – as long as you expect it. Plants of 'Rustic Dwarfs Mixed', for example, are all in the same gold/orange/mahogany/rusty-red color range and so make a most harmonious grouping, introducing a little pace into a planting without upsetting the color

Rudbeckia *'Irish Eyes' ('Green Eyes')*

Rudbeckia *'Rustic Dwarfs Mixed'*
(single)

theme. Breeders consider variation in gloriosa daisies in contrasting ways. Those developing single-flowered, dwarf varieties in pale lemon yellow are spending years ensuring that the color is uniform; another company developing a far more appealing, taller double-flowered type in rusty browns sees a degree of variation as a positive advantage – and so do I.

One of the most useful attributes of gloriosa daisies is that, apart from 'Toto' and the ignorable 'Becky', they have a highly companionable habit. The foliage is not so dense that neighbors are crowded out but, instead, allows them to sneak in among the rasping stems to provide an elegant background. The looser French marigolds, 'Coral Reef' phlox in beigey and creamy pink tones, or the old phlox 'Cream Beauty' make congenial partners. For something more startling, the flowering stems of *Verbena* 'Homestead Purple' will snake in between and then surge up to open in close and exciting companionship with the rudbeckias.

Raising rudbeckias from seed presents no special problems, although it's wise to move them into individual pots as soon as possible and give them plenty of root room to ensure that the plants develop well.

However, unlike many summer annuals they will flower fairly well even if treated badly; their recovery from being starved and constricted in small pots is remarkable. This makes them ideal for gardeners wishing to raise their own half-hardy annuals from seed and create a brilliant show yet who tend to disappear for long weekends without watering first.

Salpiglossis *Painted Tongue*

In the early 1980s I visited a British plant breeder's research station in cold and windy Norfolk. Out in the trial's field was a large square plot of what looked like hundreds of dead twigs. These were the remnants of the salpiglossis trials, and a few of these sad remains had canes pushed in alongside them as markers.

The breeder's aim was to transform the tender, Chilean-native salpiglossis from a greenhouse ornamental, or an outdoor plant for warm climates, to a summer bedding plant for cooler areas while ensuring that it could be raised in the same way as petunias. They were to be made shorter, so that strong winds actually left them standing up, and were selected for their ability to flower well in cool climates. The result of selecting these few specimens was, many years later, the Casino Series, followed more recently by the ten-color Royale Series.

The Royales have brought the sumptuous and slightly exotic painted tonuge into cooler gardens for the first time. The addition of a completely new color in the form of 'Royale Chocolate', often listed as 'Chocolate Pot', has brought new style to the dark, rich and sumptuous plantings which are now so popular.

So add 'Chocolate Pot' to dark-leaved *Hibiscus acetosella*, to rusty and deep crimson dahlias, or to *Cosmos atrosanguineus*, and the result is truly impressive. The petals have a sheen to them which adds an unexpected touch of light to the planting. And the higher profile of salpiglossis has led to the reintroduction of the long neglected, deep moody blue 'Kew Blue' which is splendid with *Salvia farinacea* 'Victoria' and 'Blue Buttons' phlox. Unfortunately, you may have to send to England for some of these varieties. 'Yellow Chilli' is a sumptuous, yet brilliant yellow from the Royale Series which has the flower power, along with the style, to be the perfect choice where a taller rich yellow is needed; other than rudbeckias there are few such options with a dependably long season. Try it with 'David Howard' dahlias whose bronze foliage and fully double orange flowers need a little airiness and grace around them, or above the coppery foliage of *Haloragis* 'Melton Bronze'.

'Royale Pale Blue Bicolor' with its pretty pattern of blue and white veining and its yellow throat requires more carefully chosen neighbors. Consider picking up the dark, almost brown throat color with *Heuchera* 'Palace Purple' or, a little more of a gamble as it needs rich soil, the perennial *Rumex flexuosus* with its snaking brown shoots and slender brown foliage.

'Gloomy Rival' must have the strangest varietal name in the history of plants. It's a strange color too – gray with brown veins and brown throat. This is best as a modest clump near the path with purple-leaved shrubs in the background.

Because painted tongues make plants which grow large quickly, as soon as they're growing strongly they're best moved into 5 in./12.5 cm. pots where they're less likely to become potbound.

Even the most modern varieties of painted tongue tend to run up on a single stem without branching. Ensuring that the pots are well spaced as the plants develop encourages them to branch from low down and gives a superior plant.

Salpiglossis *'Royale Blue Bicolor'*

Salpiglossis *'Chocolate Pot'*

Salvia **Salvia**

Don't turn the page! You can relax. Would I advise filling your garden with salvias so savagely scarlet that you need to carry smelling salts every time you stepped outside? No, you're safe, I assure you.

That a relatively attractive Brazilian wild plant has been turned into a horticultural monstrosity, to be packed into the flower beds of public parks, surrounded by neatly alternating white alyssum and dark blue lobelia, is a discredit to a noble genus. And look in the catalogs: can you tell one from another? Grow them side-by-side in a trials field, as the big seed companies do – and it's still practically impossible.

Fortunately, dwarf bedding salvias have undergone something of a revolution recently. New colors have appeared. First deep purple, crimson and creamy white, then various pinks and mauves have been introduced in a number of series. Subsequently we were hit with striped types, and more recently with varieties whose calyx is a different color from the flower or in which the individual flowers are bicolored. They are good, but all have the same fault: they're too squat. What we need are taller, bushy varieties reaching 15 in./38 cm., 18 in./45 cm. or even 2 ft./60 cm., with a long succession of much smaller, more open spikes. We have 'Rambo' and 'Bonfire' in this vein, but we need it in all these new colors; the breeders think I'm mad.

The Salsa and Sizzler series are the best. They are early-flowering and have summer-long staying power in the open garden when cosseted; grown in containers in which they're fed, watered and deadheaded regularly they last the season with a swagger and can be

Salvia *'Rambo'*

invaluable. They also have a slightly angular habit, with the flower spikes striking off at a slant rather than being determinedly upright, and this allows other plants to sneak in between the spikes to make interesting associations. For example, the dainty zinnia relative, *Sanvitalia procumbens*, with its small, dark-centered lemon flowers is a real sparkler peeping out among the flowers of 'Sizzler Purple' then streaming over the sides of a container.

But there are at least four other salvia species, less Lilliputian in their habit, which fit sympathetically into informal annual plantings and into mixed borders. The Texan *Salvia farinacea*, also known as mealy-cup sage, with its slender tuberous roots, may come in a very restricted color range – basically it's blue or it's white – but is nevertheless an important species. The foliage is narrow, dark, and glossy; its flowering stems stand strikingly vertical and each is lined with small flowers which have the unusual habit of opening at the same time at different points along the stem. The stem itself is slightly downy, in dark blue or white.

Varieties range in height from about 15 in./38 cm. to over 2 ft./60 cm. 'Rhea' and the slightly taller 'Victoria' and the taller still 'Blue Victory' have dark blue flowers on dark blue stems; 'Cirrus' and the taller 'Victoria Silver' and then 'White Victory' have white flowers on silver stems; the neat and sparky AAS winning 'Strata' and the slightly taller 'Sea Breeze' have blue and white bicolored flowers on silver stems. Mingle them, allow them to surge through the blue and white *Browallia* 'Sapphire' in a container or border or set 'Victoria Silver' to make a sympathetic contrast

ABOVE *'Sizzler Lavender' is one of the newer salvia colors with the flower power of the reds. Here, it fronts the neat growing* Alstroemeria *'Deep Rose', the first F$_1$ hybrid type, and a single color from* Phlox *'Cecily Old and New Shades' in a mauve grouping with white highlights from the alstroemeria and phlox.*

in front of a dark-leaved dahlia such as 'Bishop of Llandaff'.

Salvia coccinea is a scarlet salvia, but in a more comely style than most red bedding salvias, which have the bloated arrogance of an undersized bouncer outside a seedy basement club. In contrast, 'Lady in Red', the pink and white 'Coral Nymph' and 'Snow Nymph' have the assured elegance of the dancers we're standing in line to see.

These three, all favorites with hummingbirds, reach about 2 ft./60 cm. and, although they start to flower a little later in the summer than other salvias, they fit so well into borders with perennials and taller, naturalistic annuals that we can forgive their late appearance.

Create a rosy harmony with 'Coral Nymph' and the tall pink and white annual phlox, 'Leopoldii'; 'Snow Nymph' may be a fraction less prolific but playing cool with pale lemon *Chrysanthemum* 'Primrose Gem' it's the only tall and elegant white form. And with 'Lady in Red' it's possible to create a more satisfying version of the tired old red, white, and blue bedding that this book is aiming to banish for good. So combine it with the sultry *Salpiglossis* 'Kew Blue' and *Cosmos* 'Sonata White'; or front it first with *Salvia farinacea* 'Blue Victory', then clouds of the trailing *Lobelia* 'Regatta Blue Splash' planted as edging with that most captivating of all bedding geraniums, the eagerly awaited 'Sensation Picotee'.

In a quite different style, and color range, is *Salvia patens*. This is a plant with modest impact but real class – the absolute antithesis of dwarf-bedding shockers such as 'Blaze of Fire'. It could hardly be said to produce a forest of growth and for much of the time each 2–3 ft./ 60–90 cm. stem may only carry two or three open flowers – but they're easily the largest of any salvias which could conceivably be used for bedding and they have an intriguing parrot-beak shape. Most forms of this slightly tuberous species are best used in containers where their flowers can be appreciated more closely.

Seed production in *Salvia patens* is an unpredictable business, especially on a commercial scale; perhaps we lack the wild pollinators found in their natural South American habitat. The result is that forms of this plant rarely appear in seed catalogs, although what little seed is produced is usually true to type.

The natural species is a bright royal blue: 'Oxford Blue' and 'Royal Blue' seem little different; 'Cambridge Blue' is a lovely clear sky shade; 'Chilcombe', named for the garden of the English painter John Hubbard where it originated, is an unusual misty mauve; 'White Trophy' is. . . of course, white, though with a faint blue smudge at the base. The only variety best grown in borders is the astonishing 'Guanajuato', a wild-collected form growing to twice the normal height and with flowers almost twice the normal size. All these are now becoming available.

The last of this important genus (which also contains several other useful species) are a true annual and three true biennials – all the rest are perennials in their natural habitats. In *Salvia horminum* (sometimes incorrectly known as clary) the color comes from the bracts. For drying or as an all-summer annual, sow outside; for more carefully planned intimate plantings, sow relatively late indoors in pots rather than trays.

The profoundly silvered rosettes of the biennials *Salvia argentea* and the more cut-leaved *S. aethiopis* are irresistible at the front of well-drained sunny borders – they just demand to be touched. But they can be difficult to accommodate since their flower stems stretch up to 2 ft./60 cm. high in late spring and summer, and their flowers are rather open in form and not quite dense enough to be overwhelming or impressive; they sometimes seem uncomfortable in such a position. Then they die and leave an ugly gap – eventually filled with their own seedlings.

Better suited to the back of the border is the true clary, *S. sclarea*. This is a chunkier plant with much larger rosettes in dark green and with a noticeable network of veining. It enjoys the same sunny site and well-drained soil but produces surging stems with, again, relatively insignificant flowers with bold bracts attached. These bracts hang down beneath the flower and can be purple or, more striking in var. *turkestanica*, white with purple tints.

You may be skeptical about my enthusiasm for some salvias, but clary is one which even the most unreconstructed banisher of bedding can enjoy.

Salvia farinacea *'Blue Victory'* and *'White Victory'*

Salvia patens *'Cambridge Blue'*

Salvia argentea

RIGHT *The long-lasting color in this purplish-blue form of* Salvia viridis *is provided by bracts, leafy structures around the flowers, which provide color in cream with green veins, blue, or pink; the tiny two-lipped flowers are relatively insignificant. With the unruly and ever-changing double Shirley poppies around them, the upright stems bring an air of calm in spite of their bold coloring.*

Tagetes *Marigold*

I hate marigolds. Well, says he quickly, I don't hate them all, for such sweeping scorn would make this chapter singularly unhelpful. Just bear with me while I say my piece before I come to some of the most valuable and stylish of all garden annuals. But really, why grow African marigolds? If a truck backed up to your gate and tipped out a huge load of those yellow playballs you see at nursery schools, would you arrange them in your borders? If a salesman called at your door and offered you plastic oranges on sticks, would you plant them neatly in your containers?

You get my point. African marigolds may be colorful but so is paint. And the heads of the Discovery (discover how horrid they are), Sumo (as bloated as you'd expect), and Perfection (perfectly ghastly) Series marigolds are jammed together so tightly that you might as well have bought them by the yard from Home Depot and rolled them out like carpet. This is the only time when you could possibly be grateful for botrytis.

So, having written off one of the four main groups of marigolds, do they have any more desirable relations? Of course. There are French marigolds, there are the triploid hybrids, and there are "tagetes" *Tagetes*.

In French marigolds, eschew all the unnaturally tiny varieties like 'Boy O'Boy'

Tagetes 'Seven Star Red'

Tagetes 'Mischief Mahogany'

(how could you do otherwise), and concentrate on two particular groups of varieties: the rusty doubles and the taller singles.

The rusty and mahogany doubles, often insulted with the appellation "red", can be gorgeous; 'Scarlet Sophie' is the best (but by no means scarlet). Brighter shades with the vibrancy of 'Safari Tangerine' are difficult to place - though pink verbena is a possible companion . . . !

The taller single French marigolds are both more elegant and more adaptable and, in private gardens, where plants are carefully tended, you can often add 25% to the heights given in catalogs. Two series stand out, Favorite and Mischief. The former is easier to find but I'm afraid I prefer the latter.

The Favorites come in five colors, Mischief in six, of which the mahogany with its finest of yellow wiring round the petals is the pick. Peeping through the lemon-lime leaves of *Helichrysum petiolare* 'Limelight', it's unexpectedly stunning; with the unusual bronze of *Haloragis erecta* 'Melton Bronze' and the fleeting yellow stars of *Bulbine annua* on their juicy green stems it's surprisingly refined. They are rarely available in separate colors, so grow them to first flower, then make a selection for planting.

Of all the French marigolds, the recently revived

RIGHT *The essence of good bedding. Thoughtfully grouped plants in ones, twos and threes mingle together as the season progresses. The supposedly double-flowered Rudbeckia 'Goldilocks' has many buds still to open and 'Golden Gem' tagetes, darker than 'Primrose Gem', melds in well colourwise. In front, the mahogany in the stripes of 'Dwarf Harlequin' marigolds, much like 'Legion of Honour' from the nineteenth century, picks up the dark eyes of the rudbeckias and the rarely seen foliage of Haloragis erecta 'Wellington Bronze', a real find, holds it all together. Great!*

LEFT *'Primrose Gem' is the coolest of all the tagetes; snaking in alongside the sympathetically cream-variegated yellow loosestrife,* Lysimachia punctata *'Alexander'. With a darker element added by* Cryptotaenia japonica f. atropurpurea, *the combination of contrast and harmony is singularly appealing. The close planting stretches its otherwise densely rounded mounds, which can be tricky to fit with other, more relaxed plants.*

Victorian striped forms are the most choice; modern names like 'Striped Marvel' have replaced originals like 'Harlequin' and 'Old Scotch Prize'. The Victorians grew singles and doubles, tall and short, some with a single mahogany stripe through each petal, some striped at the edges. They were rarely illustrated in old catalogs and the simple description "beautifully striped" failed to distinguish them.

The taller forms are the best. Reaching 2–3 ft./60–90 cm. and excellent for cutting, their flowers are carried on long stems with an unexpected airiness. They mingle contentedly in mixed borders with yellow grasses or sedges like *Carex stricta* 'Aurea'; they fit into temporary summer plantings in front of dark-leaved dahlias; they color match *Calendula* 'Indian Prince' in strictly annual plantings. The one problem is that flowers which develop under stress may temporarily lose their stripes.

For simple flowering power the hybrids between the African and the French marigolds cannot be beat; they might also give you a headache, some are so unnervingly bright, but they are prolific. Known as triploid, Afro-French, or Super French marigolds, they seldom produce seed and flower prolifically without deadheading.

Tagetes 'Seven Star Red' is gorgeous. Its deep mahogany flowers slowly become rustier, then more orange, but it's a harmonious fading. Try it with tightly curled 'Pagoda' parsley, with a trailing bidens like 'Golden Eye', with *Coprosma* 'County Park Purple' (a glossy-leaved, bronzy New Zealand shrub

worth searching out), or with *Rudbeckia* 'Goldilocks'.

The so-called "tagetes" can be difficult to use in the garden. Occasionally, they're seen in a dwarf hedge lining a path to a cottage door but are so dominant that plants behind are visually overwhelmed. One answer is to use them with close neighbors like painted tongue which will disrupt their form by surging through them, or with rudbeckias which are sufficiently robust to break up their slightly suffocating growth.

The pure colors, like the helpfully descriptive 'Primrose Gem', 'Paprika', and 'Golden Gem', are the most effective. All have that sharp, fresh scent to their finely cut foliage which makes weeding among them a pleasure – although their dense growth usually smothers weeds before they become established.

ABOVE LEFT *Fragrances come together in this end-of-season combination. The marigold is an unusual one: 'Tessy' is a hybrid between what is usually referred to as a "tagetes" (Tagetes tenuifolia) and a French marigold, and retains some of the scent of the former in its foliage. Surging though are the waiting-to-shed seedheads of dill, Anethum graveolens.*

ABOVE *Even the russet tones of 'Scarlet Sophie' marigolds could be a little too truculent in some plantings, especially as they become more orange as they fade. Here, softened by the cool foliage and flower of 'Tip Top Apricot' nasturtiums and the unpredictable wavy wands of the bronze-leaved* Rumex flexuosus, *they look just great. They last into winter if deadheaded regularly and, like most marigolds, a quick tug on a fading flower removes it cleanly.*

Tanacetum *Feverfew*

Feverfew has two valuable features: foliage and quick-from-seed flowers. The yellow-leaved feverfew, *Tanacetum parthenium* 'Aureum', is one of those much-appreciated plants which deserves more attention in the American garden. Once arrived it's enjoyed – except where it becomes invasive. The form 'Gold Ball' makes neat little yellow domes but, in succeeding self-sown generations, it stretches and matures into an altogether more elegant plant. The yellow leaves (not 'gold', please) are invaluable and its white daisies too; the leaves are fragrant, the stems good for cutting and it deserves to be treated with more respect than simply allowed to self-sow.

But there are more feverfews, plenty more – although they can be hard to find unless you order seed from England. The Dutch have raised a succession of forms intended as cut flowers; some, like 'Virgo', have clean, cream-eyed white buttons, while 'Santana' is more intentionally yellow. Reaching 2–3 ft./60–90 cm., 'Virgo' makes a fine border plant with the dusky red spikes of *Veronica spicata* 'Rotfuchs', and in well-drained soil all of these forms will behave as short-lived, first-summer-flowering, perennials.

There are few good seed-raised, silver-leaved annuals, but *Tanacetum ptarmiciflorum*, sometimes unnecessarily overdignified with the variety name 'Silver Feather', is one with a great character. It never flowers the first summer but its flat, pewter gray foliage, finely and prettily dissected, is a fine companion in containers with diascias, twiggy nemesias, and other not-too-pugnacious plants. Unless started inconveniently early, it rarely makes a good-sized plant in the less pampered conditions of the bed or border.

Feverfew, I should say, is so-called from its traditional use as a medication against fever and colds. Botanically, the yellow-leaved and cut-flower types have in the past been assigned to both *Matricaria* and *Chrysanthemum* while the silver-leaved type has usually been billeted in *Pyrethrum*; now, all are classified as *Tanacetum*.

LEFT *The fresh foliage of yellow-leaved feverfew,* Tanacetum parthenium *'Aureum', creates a bright speck of sunlight all winter, then stretches before revealing its white daisies. Planted, as here, with the deep purple heads of* Allium sphaerocephalon *falling through it, or self-sown in happy, and sometimes less than happy combinations, the sharp fragrance of its leaves is released as you remove unwanted seedlings or simply brush against it.*

Tithonia Mexican Sunflower

Strong and vigorous annuals which create a real presence in a border are becoming increasingly uncommon as plant breeders strive to reduce everything to the size of a French marigold. There are signs that the magnificent *Tithonia rotundifolia*, a Mexican native, which I've grown to 6 ft./1.8 m., may be destined for this treatment. But why turn a unique plant into an approximation of a commonplace and characterless one?

Tithonia is a boisterous, rough-and-ready plant, heat-loving and drought-tolerant, with flowers rather like those of a single dahlia, orange-red in color with a yellow eye; it's an ideal component of hot-color fall borders. 'Torch' is a little shorter and bushier while 'Goldfinger', at 3 ft./90 cm. is even shorter yet still an effective plant. The orange-tinted 'Yellow Torch' seems to have disappeared but may well be the same as 'Sunset' and 'Aztec Gold'. I was dreading the development of even shorter varieties and now, with the arrival of 'Fiesta del Sol', that most feared prophecy has come to pass. This 12 in./30 cm. tithonia has all the floral elegance of an orange brick – so throw it through the seed company's window. If you need a dwarf variety in orange or yellow, please choose a rudbeckia or even a marigold.

With so few really substantial seed-raised plants available, 'Goldfinger' and 'Torch' are invaluable components of larger annual plantings. Dark-leaved dahlias or amaranthus could go alongside, taller rudbeckias could go in front and canary vine (*Tropaeolum peregrinum*) could sprawl through. 'Goldfinger' would look very fine with *Mina lobata*, but, as it is not sufficiently robust to take the mina's weight, the vine would have to be planted on the fences behind and trail forward into the tithonia.

Such is the vigor of Mexican sunflowers that they're best sown in early spring, pricked out into 3 in./7 cm. pots, then moved into 5 in./12.5 cm pots so that the roots never become too restricted; they will branch if not crowded in their early stages. In exposed sites, stake the main stem, as the broad leaves catch the wind effectively.

LEFT *'Goldfinger' is here planted around an established clump of the large-flowered* Crocosmia *'Star of the East' and creates an unexpected harmony of flower colors, together with an intriguing contrast in foliage. The tithonia will continue to flower well into fall and also become increasingly bushy, hiding the ragged end-of-season leaves of the crocosmia after its flowers are over.*

Tropaeolum Nasturtium and Canary Vine

There was a time in Britain not so long ago when the more snobbish looked down on nasturtiums – and sneered. Some still do. In America, of course, things are different. There's a much more egalitarian and less class-ridden attitude to plants, and nasturtiums are accepted for what they are – valuable, if unexpectedly fussy plants.

The climbing sorts, however, seem least particular; these are the most closely related to their wild South American ancestors and they certainly can grow. In recent years we've been limited to those with such dispiriting names as 'Climbing Mixed', but, fortunately, a few remain from their Victorian heyday, including the pale lemon 'Moonlight' and the poetically named 'Jewel of Africa' with its prettily marbled leaves.

If you start them off in 3 in./7 cm. pots and plant under evergreen hedges, the seedlings remain sufficiently starved to give a good account of themselves. Starving is crucial: feed them and water them as you do your family when they come for Thanksgiving and nasturtiums will react in the same way; they'll expand heartily, then begin to look rather green . . . and their less appealing characteristics will eventually emerge.

Given conditions which are too rich, it's always said that nasturtiums produce leaves at the expense of flowers; what actually happens is that the petioles, the leaf stems, grow longer than they do in more Spartan conditions, so the sandwich-sized leaves simply hide the flowers. At the base of an established hedge or shrub, which will suck up most of the water and nutrients, the balance is often better and the show a fine one. Plant them under a wigwam of canes in a richly manured flower bed and they will romp to the top, a juicy, leafy spire – then a gale will blow them all over.

Bushy nasturtiums are similar: rich fare produces luxuriant leaves. Fortunately their leaves are among the most striking of all annuals but the flowers will still be hidden if the soil is too rich. If you add humus to your flower bed, leave some unimproved; if you spread fertilizer, leave an area untreated. Then make a sign: here be nasturtiums.

Breeders have been aiming for bushy varieties which hold their flowers above their leaves, even in rich conditions. The Whirlybird Series is the best so far, the flowers spurless and held up to face the viewer. 'Alaska Mixed' is second class in this respect – but its speckled foliage is superb; the new 'Tutti Frutti' has a better blend of flower colors. The old dark-leaved

Tropaeolum *'Whirlybird Scarlet'*

ABOVE LEFT *In spite of the mass of fluted yellow provided by the 'Primrose Jewel' nasturtiums, doesn't this simple combination have a quiet coolness about it? The flowers of* Nemesia *'Bluebird', brightly contrasting in color yet content to be overwhelmed in scale, mingle with the nasturtium in a quietly confident way, so different from the brashness of much annual planting.*

varieties also score more on foliage than habit; the wonderful 'Empress of India' is the only variety which is far more dependably bushy.

All this talk of strong and luxuriant growth might lead you to believe that nasturtiums are easy to grow; but no; they're martyrs to pests. Black aphids, leaf miners, flea beetle, plus pea and bean weevil can all be devastating – and nasturtiums are also unexpectedly sensitive to many insecticides. I now use a systemic insecticide every week – but at half-strength to prevent the leaves being damaged. It works.

ABOVE LEFT *Perhaps the best hosts for annual climbers are other climbers. Here,* Clematis. x jouiniana *with its dark foliage and blue-tinted white flowers, supports the long trails of canary vine,* Tropaeolum peregrinum. *The spikes of red buds and creamy flowers of* Mina lobata *are perhaps more striking.* Mina *may need heat to start it off but it is worth the effort.*

ABOVE *The old style 'Peach Melba' with the red blotch, and the pure yellow of 'Primrose Jewel' sprawl through the delicate gray* Senecio viravira. *The clean lines of the neatly dissected senecio foliage are set against the rounded nasturtiums and the speckled leaves of* Tolmiea menziesii *'Taff's Gold'.*

165

Verbena **Verbena**

Verbenas are a surprisingly mixed bunch. Most are neat and perhaps even a little blocky in habit, although few are so tight and rigid as to exclude their inquisitive neighbors from intermingling to create happy associations. The one unexpectedly tall and wirily slender species is also a blender by nature. And verbenas boast both rich velvet shades and cool pastels.

The Sandy, Novalis and Romance Series, forms of *Verbena* x *hybrida*, all are compact and rather upright, 10–12 in./25–30 cm. high, with flowers gathered in a horizontal plane at the top of the plant; all are susceptible to mildew (though spraying usually works) and they germinate poorly. However, the color range is superb, especially in the Romance Series, and the colors so cool or intoxicating that they beg indulgence. The palest lavender pink of 'Romance Lavender' is delightful with the sympathetic silvery trails of *Plecostachys serpyllifolia*. The Quartz Series boasts the best germination; 'Quartz Burgundy' is a distinctive deep shade, great with *Perilla frutescens* 'Atropurpurea', the deep purple-leaved shiso; *Verbena* 'Blue Lagoon', by far the best blue, also appreciates this sultry purple-leaved neighbor. 'Peaches and Cream' has a unique coloring and is lovely with *Phlox* 'Cream Beauty'; interplanted with the delicate *Platystemon californicus* peeping out among the flower heads, it's a treat. But its germination is poor.

The award-winning 'Imagination', which was derived from *Verbena tenuisecta*, has an arching, spreading habit, finely dissected

Verbena *'Peaches and Cream'*

foliage, clouds of smaller, deep purple flowers, and less mildew. It's stunning with the dainty yellow buttons of *Sanvitalia procumbens* running through it.

'Polaris', a form of *V. rigida*, is probably the prettiest color of all verbenas – a warmly icy, soft lilac-blue – but is difficult to find in catalogs. Although reaching 12–14 in./30–35 cm., 'Polaris' is less congested than the more widespread bedding types and makes a cool combination with small blue hostas like 'Halycon'. Its progenitor, *V. rigida* (often listed as *V. venosa*) may be familiar from municipal displays; interplanted with red geraniums it creates a shimmering purple haze above the bright scarlet flowers. This works even better on a more intimate scale. The cooler counterpart of those colors is 'Polaris' in concert with 'Vogue Appleblossom' geraniums.

The most fashionable verbena among plant lovers is *V. bonariensis*. Stiff and absolutely vertical, it makes 4–5 ft./1.2–1.5 m with its purple flowers gathered at the top. This is a good perennial in many areas but flowers well in its first year from seed. It's superb set at the very front of a border where you look through it like a sparse curtain to the plantings behind, or at the back interplanted with the tall and fiery red-hot pokers, *Kniphofia* 'Prince Igor'. Sow the dainty yellow *Tropaeolum peregrinum* to clamber through them all. Once you have it, probably you always will, for *V. bonariensis* self-sows freely. In addition, this is the one verbena which germinates easily.

Germination is a problem with

most verbenas owing to the almost impermeable waxy layer immediately under the seed coat. But keeping the seed moist in an attempt to compensate is a mistake, as verbena seed germinates poorly in damp mix. Instead, prepare the seed pots and water the potting mix the day before sowing. Then sow the seed and cover either with vermiculite or dry seed-starting mix and keep it in the dark at 65–70°F/18–21°C until germination; higher temperatures can also be inhibiting. Keep relatively dry until the seedlings are growing well.

BELOW *Intermingling plants works as well with tall, substantial varieties as it does with more compact types, provided enough space is available. Here,* Nicotiana sylvestris *has been interplanted with* Verbena bonariensis, *the wiry stems of the verbena standing out against the nicotiana's broad foliage, and the haze of purple enlivened by the glints of the white flowers of the tobacco plant. 'Purity' or 'Pied Piper Red' cosmos also make good companions.*

Viola *Pansy and Violet*

We all have an urge to deal with large quantities of information by organizing and classifying it. We group together material which has clearly distinguishable common features and separate it from other groups with different factors in common. If only it were that simple with pansies and violas.

Of course, they all have the same distinctive flower structure. Unfortunately, they vary so much in their other features, and have so many intermediates, that classifying them is almost impossible. True, it is possible to correlate four main features: flower size, leaf size, degree of branching, and rate of flower production. As a rule, large flowers go with large leaves, sparse branching and a modest rate of flower production; small flowers go with small leaves, repeated branching and prolific flowering.

But it's the vast range of in-betweens which muddle the issue between the larger pansies and the smaller violas. With terms like Mini-Pansy, Miniola, Large-Flowered Viola, and Small-Flowered Pansy blurring the edges between what were once clearly distinct groups, it's best to invoke some personal criteria, the better to reduce the range to manageable proportions.

First, I must exclude most of those primarily intended for summer flowering. We have enough flowers for summer and too few for spring, so

Viola *'Padparadja'* with Tulipa *'Giuseppe Verdi'*

Viola *'Jackanapes'*

Viola *'Bowles' Black'*

transforming pansies from their natural spring flowering period into summer flowers is to be discouraged. The Imperial and Accord series are therefore excluded, in spite of the subtle and startling color combinations in the former. Let's also exclude those boasting flowers larger than those of the familiar Universal Plus, Maxim and Crystal Bowl and Ultima series (about 2 in./5 cm.). Large flowers are a disadvantage in pansies: they're disproportionate to the size of the plant on which they're carried and the tissue of the petals is often insufficiently robust to support their weight; the edges collapse, giving the flowers a ragged look. So the Super Majestic Colossal Giants (I kid you not), Crown, Royal, Happy Face, Majestic, Mammoth Giants, and Atlas series are all excluded. I feel better already.

Most pansies and violas are produced in series, some of which, like the Ultima Series, a blend of the Maxim and Crystal Bowl series, can run to almost thirty colors. Catalogs tend to offer mixtures, either of all the colors in the series, or color-themed mixtures selected from the series, such as the pastel 'Silhouette', plus a few exceptional separate colors. I would always urge that you choose separates so that you can plan color associations more carefully. Pansies and violas often feature faces, blotches, eyes, or whiskers in contrasting colors,

enabling fluid and inclusive plant groupings to be created. This ability to create links with other plants in two color ranges is invaluable.

Catalogs list individual colors from larger series as well as one-of-a-kinds. 'Springtime Lemon Splash' in pale lemon with a blotch in deep blackcurrant-purple, is unique in its coloring; slipped among a permanent planting of larger daffodils like 'King Midas' and dark-leaved *Heuchera* 'Stormy Seas', it creates an invaluable cohesion.

Older one-of-a-kinds like the bicolored yellow-and-purple 'Jackanapes', named after Gertrude Jekyll's pet monkey, tend to be much looser, even sprawling in habit. 'Jackanapes' will scramble up into a purple cut-leaved maple or over and around the emerging evergreen shoots of *Cryptotaenia japonica* f. *atropurpurea* to make delightful combinations. The almost black 'Blackjack', an improved version of the old favorite 'Bowles Black', is pretty set among the

ABOVE LEFT *Early in the summer season, this 'Fanfare White Blotch' pansy is not much more than a tufty little plant among the overwintered heliotrope and the steadily increasing 'The Crocodile' ivy-leaved geranium. But in zones with mild-temperature summers, as the season advances, the pansy will fill out just as the bare stems of the geranium and heliotrope would otherwise become obtrusive, and that bare middle ground will be filled with sympathetic color, the delicate purple face of the pansy picking up the color in the flower of the heliotrope.*

ABOVE *This swarm of the slightly variable Viola tricolor 'Johnny Jump Up' – a Colonial-era favorite – is close to the wild species whose blood is in all these pansies and violas. Its consistent purple element connects it with similar shades in the dark-leaved dahlia and, in a paler range, Silene 'Rose Angel'. Sometimes listed under Viscaria, these latter are easy and underrated annuals for direct sowing whose colors have been improved in recent years. Silene 'Cherry Blossom', in white-eyed rose-pink is especially pretty.*

LEFT *Self-sown viola seedlings can be invaluable. If you don't mind their unpredictability you can let them loose among the stems of* Allium cristophii *and with the almost imperceptible clouds of bent grass,* Agrostis nebulosa, *the more solid yet decidedly lacy* Artemisia alba *'Canescens' dispatching its steadily running roots among the whole planting until the allium is set against silver and the violas mingle in front. With careful thinning of the flower colors, year by year you can manipulate the shades of the violas.*

ABOVE *Looking in close often gives you an entirely new view. The dark stems and foliage of* Anthriscus sylvestris *'Ravenswing' stretch to 3–4 ft./90 cm.–1.2 m. in height but, down at the base, the 'Ultima Pink Shades' pansy is just the right color to create a little gleam among those dark stems and leaves, without a stark contrast.*

bright yellow leaves of *Lysimachia nummularia* 'Aurea' or white grape hyacinths.

Most violas will trail if given the opportunity; truly trailing types are the next development. The tiny yellow 'Sunbeam' is delightful in a basket, though hardly flamboyant, and also makes a very pretty ground cover with the tiniest of purple crocus, *C. sieberi* 'Violet Queen' perhaps, peeping through. Look for its larger-flowered successors like 'Purple Rain'.

The Ultima, Universal Plus, Springtime, and Delta series flower in the autumn, mild spells in winter, and are at their peak in spring; the mixtures are far easier to find than separates. Simply filling a windowbox or trough with a sparkling mixture can be very cheerful but since plants will often be carrying their first flowers at planting time you can select by color for more thoughtful planting. For example, pick out the blue-and-white bicolored 'Maxim Marina' or 'Universal Plus Marina' to go with a blend of blue and white *Muscari azureum*.

But the smaller the flowers, the better I like them, and the easier they are to accommodate with dwarf bulbs and spring perennials. While 'Fanfare', described as a Large-Flowered Viola or a Floribunda Pansy, and 'Velour', described as a Mini-Pansy, may have some superb individual colors, neither has as wide a range as the smaller-flowered Sorbet Series of violas, whose twelve colors, many in delightful combinations, are perfect with dwarf bulbs. This series is a triumph. 'Sorbet Blueberry Cream', with its continuous succession of neat flowers in pale lavender blue, with gold on the lower lip and short dark whiskers, could be set among *Crocus tommasinianus*; 'Sorbet Blackberry Cream' has purple edges to a white flower and a neat yellow eye which makes *Narcissus* 'Hawera' an ideal companion.

RIGHT *Nestling at the front of this spring border, at the base of a taller planting of perennials,* Viola *'Baby Lucia', one of the first of the modern seed-raised violas, is set around the emerging shoots of the perennial* Lobelia *'Queen Victoria'. Alongside, recently planted and just taking hold, is purple-leaved basil and this harmony of coloring, created from a disparate group of plants and set against a green background, is typical of imaginative small garden planting.*

There is, though, one difficulty in growing pansies and violas for autumn and spring: seed must be sown in early summer. This may seem very convenient as space will be available after all the summer flowers are planted. But pansies germinate poorly in high temperatures and keeping them cool is difficult. A temperature of 60–65°F/15–18°C is ideal; germination drops off above 65°F/18°C, so choose a cool shady place outside for the seed pots. Rich potting mixes can also cause problems, so use a specific seed mix, rather than a potting or multi-purpose mix which contains more nutrients, and soak it well with fungicide the day before sowing as a protection against damping off.

Move the seed pots into good light as soon as the seeds germinate, as they can stretch quickly, and prick out into trays or 2½ in./6 cm. pots to grow on. Overwatering leads to a loose and flabby plant, so be cautious, and keep the plants cool – they can be stood outside once established in their pots. An occasional low-nitrogen liquid fertilizer is useful.

Zinnia Zinnia

The British just don't know what they're missing. They can't grow decent zinnias and so they imperiously look down on zinnias as somehow beneath their consideration. But here, where we have the sun zinnias love, we relish the purity of their colors and the variety of their flower forms.

Of the larger flamboyant types the Sun and Splendor series and, named with admirable frankness, 'Big Red Hybrid' with its 6 in./15 cm. flowers, are undeniably spectacular – the purity of their colors unrivaled. As cut flowers they're easy to grow and prodigiously productive.

Smaller-flowered, less traditional zinnias like the daintier, narrow-leaved *Zinnia peruviana* and *Z. angustfolia*, both in an increasing range of forms, look far more relaxed. The delicate 9 in./23 cm. Star Series in orange, yellow, white and the 'Starbright' mixture are exceptionally easy to grow, tolerate drought, are the most heat-resistant of all zinnias, flower for months and have an unusually open habit making companionable neighbors with camissonias or linarias like 'Gemstones'.

'Persian Carpet', developed from *Z. haageana*, sits between these and the large-flowered group both in plant and flower size; its neat double flowers come in warm, exotic yellow, gold, orange, and rust shades with some maroon, plum, white, and rose in a huge range of color combinations. It thrives sown direct in a sunny place and for dry banks is supreme.

There's now a more contemporary take on this intermediate range, combining neat habit with clear colors and exceptional flower production. First came the well-known Peter Pan Series in nine colors, then the more reliably double Dashers, then the more disease-resistant, six-color Pulcino Series and now the exceptionally impressive Profusion Series which is still developing.

All make attractively rounded plants, ideal for large containers, with double flowers in clear bright or soft pastel colors. They can be a little tight in their habit so require neighbors which will break down their concentrated growth into a little more informality in the garden: 'Profusion Cherry' is good with *Helichrysum petiolare*, 'Peter Pan Flame' with 'Mr. Majestic' French marigolds.

In general, sowing seed where the plants are to flower is usually more successful than sowing in pots and pricking out; the lack of disturbance ensures better establishment. Delay sowing until about a week before the last frost date in your area. Sow in damp furrows (page 179), placing the conveniently large seeds 2–3 in./5–7.5 cm. apart, then thin them out as advised on the seed packet. All groups respond well to this simple approach.

You may need to sow indoors in the coolest or overcast zones where the rate of growth during the summer months may not allow a sufficiently long period of flowering; likewise, if you need to place them precisely in the border among established plants. This requires care. Zinnia seedlings, especially those of the more flamboyant kinds, are notorious – show them a mere molecule of damping off disease and they keel over like the bridegroom at a bachelor party. Do not use 100% peat mixes, improve the drainage by adding up to 50% perlite and restore the nutrient balance by mixing in granules of slow-release container fertilizer.

Sow the seeds singly in individual cells, then cover with ¼ in./6 mm. of mix. and

Zinnia peruviana

RIGHT *The smaller-flowered zinnias like this 'Persian Carpet' are among the most adaptable, partly because they're variable but within a clearly confined color range. Here, with* Tagetes signata *'Lulu' and the neat poms of yellow ageratum,* Lonas annua, *at front and back, they add depth to a basically yellow planting.*

germinate at 70°F/21°C. Watering from below is preferable. As soon the mix in the cells is sufficiently full of roots to hold together, move them into 3½ in./9 cm. pots, setting the surface of the cell a little above the mix in the pot. This helps prevent rot.

Plant them out before the pot fills with roots, or move the plants into 5 in./12.5 cm. pots for later planting. After planting, soak them thoroughly then leave them unwatered; the natural vigor of the plants should ensure the roots establish well. Problems could still arise later. In cool, damp summers, rainwater collects among the petals of the larger, fully-double flowers and the result is botrytis infection; it also attacks the neck immediately behind the flower – which causes the flower to flop and may cripple the whole plant. Powdery mildew is also a very common problem in hot weather.

Choosing the relatively resistant varieties and spraying with an appropriate fungicide certainly helps, as does spacing to allow more air movement, and watering at soil level only. But the

ABOVE LEFT *A new take on formal bedding . . .* Pelargonium '*Multibloom Salmon*' *is grown by the thousand all over the world, but only at Landesgartenschau at Böblingen, Germany, would they think to combine it with* Zinnia '*Dreamland Coral*' – *and not just combine it, but interplant it. The zinnias must be well grown; if too many fail the display is ruined, but here it captures the eye and inspires admiration.*

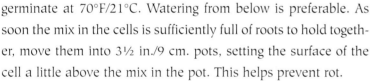

ABOVE *Backing these Persian Carpet zinnias with plants from the bigger and brighter Oklahoma Series makes a sparkling but not overwhelming combination. In front are the yellow buttons of* Lonas annua *with occasional clumps of the rich, egg-yolk yellow of* Coreopsis '*Early Sunrise*' *erupting on their vertical stems.*

smaller-flowered forms are inherently less troublesome. They also have a more natural look and insinuate better amid other plantings. Forthcoming developments will widen the range and make them even more desirable. I suggest you start with them.

Practicalities

Whether an annual is hardy or half-hardy depends on whether it can be sown directly outdoors or whether it must be started indoors first. This is not as straightforward as it sounds. The range of temperatures at which it will germinate well and produce the highest proportion of good seedlings varies from plant to plant. In any given climatic zone some annuals must be raised in the warmth of protected conditions, whereas some will germinate well when sown outside. While this distinction gives us the two familiar groups – hardy annuals and half-hardy annuals – the boundary between theses two groups varies according to where they're grown.

In colder zones many plants such as nicotianas must be treated as half-hardy and sown in cozy conditions in a greenhouse or propagator while in warmer regions they can be sown directly outside. A few plants, like cosmos, which are normally treated as half-hardy annuals, are sufficiently vigorous to be sown outside later in the spring when soil temperatures have increased.

Many annuals, even though tough enough to be sown outside, can be raised in the same way as half-hardy annuals to make them available in pots for careful planting in containers, or when small numbers are required for intimate plantings with other varieties. A few perfectly tough plants are raised as half-hardy annuals because their seeds are expensive and the packet contains relatively few; the percentage of losses is always higher from seeds sown in the open ground.

Seed sowing inside

You don't need to have a greenhouse to raise half-hardy annuals: many a successful garden has been planted with annuals raised on a shelf in the kitchen or on the sunroom windowsill. Nevertheless, a greenhouse is still the best environment.

The greenhouse

Any glass or polythene greenhouse is suitable, with certain provisos: it must have good ventilation and some form of heating, the glass or polythene must be clean,

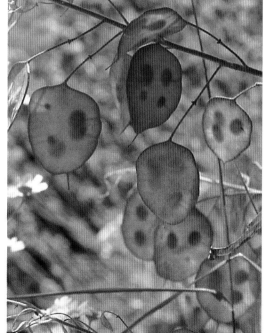

Lunaria annua *seedpods*

and, wherever possible, it should be situated to benefit from the best of the early season light.

For raising more than just a few plants, the most practical arrangement is to divide the greenhouse into a larger area, which is left unheated or given little more than frost protection, and a smaller area, which is kept warmer. The warm area can house an electric, thermostatically controlled propagator in which to germinate seeds and a second propagator in which to wean the newly germinated seedlings at a slightly lower temperature. From there they can go on to the open greenhouse bench. When raising large numbers of annuals, electric heating mats are invaluable. Always have your electricity supply fitted using waterproof sockets by a qualified electrician. Greenhouses without an electricity supply can be heated by kerosene or bottled gas, but take care with your fuels. Bottled gas heaters can be fitted without professional help but be sure to follow the instructions from the manufacturers and bottled gas suppliers. Never let kerosene heaters run low as they may fill the greenhouse with smoke.

Good shading and ventilation are vital for those spring and early summer days when the sun is strong, and you need a supply of clean tap water, not a rainwater butt, for watering. Ideally, you should fit benches with a capillary watering system to ensure that pots and trays stay constantly moist and can conveniently be left without attention.

In the house

Most annuals can adapt to less than perfect conditions indoors but it helps if the temperature is constant and the light is good. Using a propagator in a warm place is the most practical idea. Most plants don't need light the first week or two before the seedlings emerge so in most houses there are plenty of options. However, in the house or sunroom, where light may be highly directional, turn the propagator frequently, so that all the seedlings receive equal amounts of light from each side; uneven light encourages lank and unbalanced growth.

The most difficult problems arise from dealing with inadequate and strongly directional light and from trying to fit pots and trays onto shelves and windowsills and other makeshift spaces.

Timing – summer annuals

The timing of seed sowing is a tricky subject. When a delay of three weeks in sowing can make the difference between a variety flowering well and hardly flowering at all, the differences in climate between Florida or Maine, or Minnesota and San Diego, and the variation in conditions from one year to another, make it impossible to give specific advice on the best time to sow a particular variety. Most half-hardy annuals are sown in March or April, although begonias and geraniums benefit from an earlier sowing. Start by following advice on the seed packet, perhaps making adjustments according to your local practice and extension service, then adapt in the light of experiences and of extremes in seasonal conditions.

Each plant, sometimes even each variety of a plant, will flower or reach a particular size in a certain length of time from sowing under particular conditions. So, tuberous begonias, for example, should be among the first of your seeds to be sown in late winter or early spring; marigolds grow faster, so they can be sown later.

The size of the plant you need can also influence sowing time. For large containers in prominent positions, where an instant effect is a great advantage, substantial plants in flower at planting time are preferable to younger, smaller plants still waiting to flower.

There's another way of looking at it: early sowing demands extra heat to ensure that the best use is made of the additional time. This extra heat, in the coldest season, can be expensive. Planning a careful succession of varieties can minimize this expense. Unfortunately, early sowings are also the most difficult – light levels are low, days are short, and growing space may be limited – so careful daily attention is required to ensure that they thrive. Keep in mind also that if seeds are sown too early, plants will be ready to plant out before conditions in the garden allow it, so they must either be moved into larger pots, occupying additional valuable space, or they will become increasingly potbound and need more frequent watering and additional feeding. This will mean they have problems establishing when they finally go outside.

If you sow seeds too late indoors, the plants may still be small at planting time; not having grown sufficiently to thrive outdoors, they will flower late and perhaps be unable to hold their own in the rough-and-tumble of the border.

Pots and trays

Forget about standard seed trays. Long gone, except in the largest of gardens, are the days when seeds were sown in seed trays. What is the point of filling a whole seed tray with seeds that you don't really need, or spacing out the few you do need to fill an unnecessarily large area? It's simply a waste of space.

If you use 3 in./7 cm. square plastic pots instead, you'll fit 15 pots in the space occupied by a standard seed tray – and even 16 large dahlia seeds can be sown comfortably into a single pot, so you'll usually only need the one pot for each variety. Also useful are the seed trays that come ready-fitted with 3 in./7 cm. pots.

Potting mix

Never sow seeds in pots of garden soil. In the unnatural habitat of a pot in a propagator, the micro- (and not so micro-) organisms in the soil multiply quickly and many of them will attack seeds and seedlings. Garden soil also drains poorly in pots and this exacerbates disease problems. Of course, there's always the occasional gardener who raises a superb batch of semperflorens begonias in solid clay left over from excavating the foundations for the new garage – but opening the oven door is not an essential element of baking technique simply because the cake didn't fall the first time you took a look. Use fresh potting mix from the garden center.

Garden center seed- and multi-purpose potting mixes are very variable. Soil-based mixes should not be used for annuals. So, although environmental concerns prompt us to keep searching for substitutes, fertilizer-enhanced, peat-based mixes – particularly those marked "seed-starting mix" – are still the most dependable. Read the labels carefully to make sure the mix has both peat and fertilizer, since brands vary widely.

Sowing seed in pots

Make sure the potting mix is moist, then fill your seed pot loosely, tap it smartly a few times on a hard surface to settle it and wipe off any mix standing above the rim of the pot using a plant label, or something similar. Then use the bottom of another pot, or a purpose-made presser, to firm and level the mix very gently.

Cut the top off the seed packet with a pair of scissors; you'll often find a smaller packet or foil sachet inside; snip the top off this too. Don't sow all the seeds in the packet simply because they're there; consider how many plants you need.

Keep in mind too that seeds are much less likely to rot if given space to develop from the start, so sow thinly. It's impossible to be precise about this as seeds vary so much in their size and rate of development; usually the packet will give guidance. But err on the side of wide spacing and use two or even three separate pots if you need a large quantity of one variety, rather than try to cram them all into one pot.

The "tap from the packet" method is my preferred seed-sowing technique as it combines precision and control. First, make a crease halfway along one cut edge of the seed packet. Next, hold the edges of the packet between the thumb and second finger, tilt the packet slightly, and tap the edge of the packet gently with the index finger. You can then watch the seed drop off the cut edge on to the mix and adjust the rate of tapping and the movement of the packet to give an even spread. Large seeds like marigolds and zinnias can be sown individually by hand.

After sowing, cover all but the finest seed with seed-starting mix. Shake the mix through a coarse sieve made from a piece of fine mesh plastic netting tacked to a simple wooden frame; the mesh of a wire kitchen sieve is too fine. Cover the seeds with their own depth of mix; the finest seeds like begonias and lobelia are better left uncovered until germination begins and then given a light dusting of mix. Finally, label the pot with the name of the plant and the date plus, if you like, the name of the seed company.

It's often suggested that, after sowing, pots be stood in a tray of water to allow them to soak up moisture from below without disturbing the seeds on the surface. I find that as the surplus water drains away, the mix shrinks from the sides of the pot so that later, when you water from above, both water and seed wash down the gap at the side. A small watering can, fitted with a fine rose and used carefully from above is best.

Germination

Place the pots in the propagator and cover with newspaper, brown paper or a couple of sheets of greenhouse shade netting. Check every day for germination: marigolds take only a few days, lobelia takes much longer. As soon as the first tiny shoots are evident, uncover the pot to give the seedlings maximum light. It pays to cover the pots individually so that each can be uncovered as its seed germinates, leaving the rest covered. Better still, move the pots of germinating seeds into a second propagator and put more pots of freshly sown seed in the first.

After germination, the temperature can be reduced slightly. The next stage is pricking out – moving the developing seedlings to give them more space to grow without competition from their neighbors.

Pricking out

The correct stage for pricking out is usually said to be when the seedlings are large enough to handle. This is a good general guide, although it's fair to say that plants with tiny seedlings, like begonias and lobelia, will always be more difficult to handle than the larger seedlings of cosmos and calendula. Again, pots are better than seed trays for pricking out. I transfer individual seedlings into 2¼ in./ 6 cm square pots, 3 in./7 cm. pots for more vigorous varieties. Individual pots give the seedlings more mix into which to grow without competition and they can be removed for planting without root disturbance. It's also easier to fit small individual pots into a confined space.

Fill the pots in the same way as for seed sowing (see page 176). Prepare all the pots for each variety at the same time, but do not firm at all. Then carefully remove the mix and seedlings from the seed pot by sliding it out onto a hard surface, and break up the mix with your fingers to loosen the seedlings.

Using a dibber or an old pencil, make a deep hole in the center of the first pricking-out pot. Lift a good strong seedling from its mix, holding it gently by its leaves and never by its stem, then slide it into the hole so that its lowest pair of seed leaves rests on the mix. Finally, tap the pot sharply on a hard surface to settle the mix. When you've planted each batch of seedlings, water in well with a liquid fertilizer in the water (check the label for dilution rates); this will complete the settling of the mix around the seedling. Do not firm the mix, as this damages fragile roots and leads to poor drainage and damping off disease.

An increasing number of annuals are now bought as seedlings or plugs. This eliminates the tricky germination phase and allows inexperienced growers, or those with no special facilities, to raise annuals. Mail-order seedlings are often of better quality than those bought from garden centers and usually come with excellent instructions.

Growing on

Once settled, the seedlings can be grown in cooler conditions; this not only saves on the cost of heating but encourages root development rather than leafy legginess. After about six weeks, when the plant food content of most potting mixes has been exhausted, regular liquid fertilizer will be necessary; a tomato fertilizer is ideal. Avoid high-nitrogen feeds (those with a high first number) which cause lank growth.

Try to keep the plants uniformly moist. If you're concerned that they might become too spindly or too large, keep them slightly dry, but without letting them actually dry out, as this has been shown to reduce growth and increase bushiness; however, this is a technique which calls for delicate balancing.

Vigorous plants, like the taller nicotianas, asters, and zinnias as well as cosmos, annual chrysanthemums, and other naturally strong-growing plants, including climbers, may need potting on as they develop to ensure that they have sufficient room. Move them into 4 in./10 cm. or 5 in./12.5 cm. pots as necessary. There is often a temptation to pinch out the tips of seedlings to encourage bushiness but, while this can be helpful with less highly developed species, modern F_1 hybrids are bred to branch and require no pinching. Best of all, if facilities are available, simply space the plants more widely on the bench or windowsill as this in itself will encourage branching.

Some plants may need support. Tall nicotianas, cosmos, and annual chrysanthemums need a single split cane with a couple of ties. Climbers like morning glories and eccremocarpus are more difficult, as they can quickly become unwieldy with wands waving all over the place and a single stake is often insufficient. A cane in each corner of a 5 in./12.5 cm. square pot allows the stems to be wound round and tied; any that become uncontrollable can simply be shortened.

Hardening off

One of the most critical stages in raising half-hardy annuals is the transition from a protected environment to planting outside. The process, known as hardening off, involves acclimatizing the plants to increasingly cool temperatures and higher light so they eventually cope with life in the outside world. This transition is most difficult to manage when plants are raised in the house without special facilities. A divided greenhouse (see page 175) is the most practical environment. The cooler growing area can be ventilated increasingly freely from three to four weeks before planting out, then the plants moved outside from a constantly fully ventilated greenhouse area.

In the house, plants can be moved from the windowsill in a warm room to a cooler one; they can then be moved to a cool sunroom or a porch – but taking the plants straight from warm, cozy conditions and planting them outside can be fatal.

A cold frame was once an invaluable help in the hardening off process but, as gardeners have realized that a basic greenhouse can often be bought for the price of a cold frame which covers a smaller area, they've become less popular. However, in gardens where there's no space for a greenhouse, or where one would be aesthetically unsatisfactory, a wooden-sided, glass-topped frame is very useful – and can be used for growing melons once the annuals have been planted!

Seed sowing outside

The plants most frequently sown outside are hardy annuals, those which can germinate and grow in cool conditions, like alyssum and nigella. You can sow plants which are less cold-tolerant such as cosmos outside, but you will need to sow them later in the spring than hardy annuals. Both these groups are almost invariably sown where they are to flower. Biennials such as wallflowers and sweet William are also sown outside, but in summer, and are usually moved to their flowering positions in autumn; they then bloom the following year.

Conditions

Most hardy and half-hardy annuals should be sown in an open sunny place where they will flower best although in the warmest, high-sun zones some may prefer a little shade. They grow well in any soil which is not too heavy and waterlogged; their seedlings especially dislike wet soil. In wet conditions, create a friable soil structure and firm cautiously. Areas with acid rain may need to raise the soil pH with lime.

Biennials, which will be moved on to their final flowering place, need a fertile soil which holds together well – the fact that the vegetable garden is so often suggested as a good location for them indicates the right kind of soil.

Timing – hardy and half-hardy annuals

Being specific about when to sow outdoors is difficult, as this varies enormously from region to region according to the climate zone. Observing when self-sown seedlings germinate in your own garden can provide a good practical guide, as can the seed packets from your favorite seed company; the local agricultural extension service can also be of use.

Seed packets often give a range of sowing times, e.g. March to May or September to November, and this helps in two ways. It indicates that in relatively mild areas the plants will develop well from an early sowing, while in colder zones it's wise to wait; but it also shows that a late sowing will still have time to develop and flower before the season ends.

Timing – biennials

Biennials are usually sown in early summer: wallflowers, English daisies, and sweet William in the open ground; pansies, violas, and primroses in pots. My experience, especially in smaller gardens, is that all biennials are best started in pots.

In areas where plants set out in autumn may be damaged by severe winter weather (cold or wet), spring planting can be more successful. In this case, I recommend delaying sowing until mid-summer.

Preparing the soil

Soil for sowing should be fertile, though not rich; never add compost or manure immediately before sowing or in the previous autumn, unless the soil is in especially poor heart. Many annuals grow naturally in relatively impoverished conditions and, while richer fare will certainly produce more prolific and long-lasting flowers, there is a danger of promoting growth which is too lush with relatively sparse flower production. Use a balanced general fertilizer cautiously before sowing, never a high nitrogen feed.

Sowing in position

Ensure that the area where the seeds are to be sown is both weed-free and open in texture by forking the soil over to the depth of a border fork and removing any weed roots. If you need to improve the soil, fork in organic matter at this stage – old potting mix or any fine-grade, bagged soil improver is best as the nutrient levels will not be too high and the fine texture will mix easily with the soil. Firm the area well to eliminate any air pockets, then rake level, removing stones, sticks, and other debris.

It is always best to sow seeds in rows. You can then cover them with soil from between the rows without disturbing other seeds and they will germinate in distinct lines – anything not in a row is therefore clearly a weed. As the plants develop, the lines will disappear. Check the seed packet or catalog for instructions as to spacing and depth of sowing.

Use the tip of a cane, the corner of a rake, or a dibber to make small furrows (drills) in the soil as wide apart and as deep as recommended for the particular variety; if in doubt, give more space rather than less, and less depth rather than more. If the soil is dry, carefully water along the drill with the spout of a watering can, using your thumb over the spout to control the water flow. This will provide a reservoir of moisture for the young seedlings.

Open the packet as described previously (page 176) and use the same technique to sow the seeds; move the packet along the drill watching the seeds drop into the soil and ensuring that spacing is even. You can sow large seeds like zinnias or sweet peas individually to ensure the necessary spacing. Use the back of the rake to draw soil over the seeds from the side of the drills, then use the flat of the rake to gently firm the soil on top.

You can sow sunflowers and other tall annuals in clusters of three rather than in rows; after germination retain only the most vigorous seedling. Since biennials will eventually be transplanted into their flowering positions elsewhere, you can simply sow them in straight rows in the vegetable garden or any bright corner.

Immediately after germination, remove weeds from between the rows – by hoeing if the rows are sufficiently widely spaced, otherwise by hand. You must also remove weeds from within the rows, pulling them by hand, and you can remove (thin) crowded seedlings at the same time. Check the seed packet or catalog for advice on the eventual spacing. Thin first to one quarter of the eventual spacing; then, a few weeks later, reduce the number of seedlings to half those eventually required; then, in another few weeks, the last thinning can be to the final spacing.

Planting out

Most plants raised as half-hardy annuals should be planted out as soon as possible after your last frosts. In some ways, of course, this is a preposterous recommendation: how can you possibly know which frost is the last? Your experience, and that of your neighbors, as well as advice from your local agricultural extension agent, will guide you but it's worth remembering that the lie of the land and the configuration of the garden can make a significant impact on where the last light frosts actually bite.

In general, the last week of May is a safe time in most areas, although in colder parts of the country and cold gardens, allowing an extra week or two is advisable. In warmer or sheltered gardens, plants can go out in early May; more tropical zones will have even greater leeway. It is also worth bearing in mind that some plants are more frost resistant than others: snapdragons, for example, are tougher than begonias.

Biennials are usually put out in late September or early October. The problem at this end of the season is that summer flowers may still be looking good – but biennials must be allowed time to establish before winter; sometimes you may have to be ruthless to make room for them.

Preparation

In general, half-hardy annuals can take richer conditions than hardy annuals but the soil preparation can be the same as for sowing hardy annuals (see page 178). In some cases, you may want to plant your pot-raised half-hardys singly or in small groups among other plants so you should prepare individual planting places.

To prepare the plants, gather them together after hardening off and give them a generous liquid fertilizer to help them develop new root growth promptly.

Planting

Whether you're planting a few single plants, or a whole display devoted entirely to annuals, set out all the plants in position in their pots before planting any of them. Then take a step back, and consider whether they really are in their best positions. Having settled on where, exactly, they are to go, small plants can be planted with a trowel while you may find it easier to plant those in larger pots with a spade. After planting, water each plant with more liquid fertilizer – much of which will soak into the soil beneath the plant ready for when its roots start to stretch.

Plant pot-raised biennials as above. Those raised in the open should be lifted carefully – preserving as much soil as possible on their roots – and moved quickly to their flowering positions. In spring schemes, always plant the biennials first and bulbs afterwards - so that you avoid spearing the bulbs with the trowel as you plant the biennials.

Aftercare

Planting annuals in the garden is only the beginning. In an unpredictable climate, their aftercare must be tailored to the season and to the individual requirements of each variety as it thrives or languishes. No two seasons are ever quite the same.

Watering and fertilizing

Overhead watering can be as brutal as a thunderstorm; using a soaker hose eliminates this problem and is also far more water-efficient. Put it in place immediately after planting, use it infrequently but leave it on long enough to provide a thorough soaking and except in areas of drought or high heat, extra watering will probably not be necessary. No further feeding should be required during the whole season – unless individual plants are used as gap fillers later in the season, when a thorough drench, or perhaps two, with liquid fertilizer is all that is necessary.

Support

Climbing annuals obviously require support from trellis, netting, a wigwam of canes, some more elaborate wooden or steel support, or they may use other plants. It's important that the supports be in place before planting; setting them in afterwards may damage roots. Some other annuals may also require support. The taller nicotianas, cosmos, snapdragons, and annual chrysanthemums, together with cleomes, amaranthus, China asters, hollyhocks, and sunflowers may all benefit from support and usually a single stake with two or three ties is sufficient.

In windy or wet areas where shorter plants are subject to damage, plastic pea-and-bean netting spread horizontally and kept taught between stout stakes is highly effective.

Deadheading

Regular and thorough deadheading makes more impact on a display of annuals than anything else except water. However, some annuals are easier to deal with than others. The flowers of bedding lobelia are almost impossible to deadhead individually; a thorough drench to encourage regrowth followed by a quick snip with the shears is about all that's possible. Plants with larger flowers, like China asters, are much simpler and flower-cutting scissors, which grip the stem after cutting, are often easier to use than pruners.

It's worth taking the trouble to deadhead some seemingly tricky plants thoroughly. Annual phlox, nemesias, and linarias all benefit enormously from a little careful attention from the kitchen scissors.

Pests and diseases

In general, annuals are relatively free of pests and diseases but damping off and aphids are especially troublesome and others may also be damaging.

Aphids Aphids, in various shades, are universal. If present in the greenhouse on mature plants these insects will quickly move to the smallest of seedlings; they will also colonize a wide variety of annuals in the garden.

Keeping more mature plants pest-free over the winter is a good first step, as is lining the ventilators with fine mesh to keep insects out. In the garden, useful preventatives include growing plants like buckwheat, *Limnanthes douglasii,* and bushy annual convolvulus which all attract hover-flies, whose larvae are among the aphid's most voracious predators. Horticultural oil or neem sprays are also effective.

Botrytis This is usually only a problem in wet seasons on double flowers like zinnias, African marigolds and dahlias. A fluffy gray mold grows on the soggy flowers; picking off the damaged flowers promptly is the best cure.

Caterpillars Many different caterpillars attack many different plants. Columbines and geraniums are often the most severely affected, but the culprit, the victim, and the severity varies from garden to garden, region to region. Simply picking caterpillars off can often be treatment enough, otherwise *Bacillus thuringiensis* biological control is usually effective.

Damping off The main symptom of this destructive disease is the collapse of seedlings at the surface of the seed-starting mix; the disease usually starts in one area then spreads to the rest of the seedlings. Germinating seeds can also be damaged; they start to germinate, then cease to grow – then rot. There are two main factors which promote infection: poor hygiene and waterlogging.

Always use clean equipment, fresh seed-starting mix and clean tap water to avoid introducing infection, and avoid overfirming and overwatering. Wash out the watering can regularly with a fungicide known to kill these organisms; not all do – liquid copper is the usual standby. This can be watered onto the mix after sowing, during germination, and after pricking out, but take care not to overwater the mix in your eagerness to give fungicide protection.

Earwigs Chewed petals on double dahlias and zinnias are often signs of earwig damage. Earwigs hide in dark places during the day so can easily be trapped in rolls of corrugated paper. You can also spray the flowers with insecticide at dusk.

Leaf miner Columbines and chrysanthemums are the main victims of these tiny grubs which tunnel under the surface of leaves. You can pick off the unsightly leaves, squashing the grubs between thumb and finger, or use a systemic insecticide to deal with them.

Powdery mildew A fungus disease most common in hot conditions, wherein a white powdery coating develops on the leaves which eventually turn dry and crisp and then die. Plants can be killed or are often severely weakened. Plants affected include zinnias, verbena, alyssum, bachelor's buttons, and calendula. Choose resistant varieties when these are available (principally in zinnias and verbenas) although resistance may not be total. Spray with an appropriate fungicide.

Red spider mite A pest of dry climates and dry seasons; pale mottling of the leaves is followed by fine webbing around the plants. In the greenhouse these mites can spread from mature plants to seedlings and they also occur outside in warmer regions and warmer seasons. Keep the greenhouse atmosphere moist as temperatures

rise and use *Phytoseiulus persimilis* biological control.

Rust This disease affects a number of plants including snapdragons, geraniums, China asters, annual chrysanthemums, columbines, salvia, and hollyhocks; deep brown or rusty red spots appear on the underside of the foliage which is soon killed. Rust can wipe out snapdragons in a couple of weeks. There are no rust-resistant varieties. Always use a preventative fungicide which kills rusts (not all do).

Slugs and snails These are beasts. In the greenhouse they sneak out in the dead of night and munch through your seedlings leaving little but flimsy stumps behind. In the garden they will start at one end of a row of seedlings and chomp through to the other – then find the end of the next row and start back the other way. Biological control is partially effective, but expensive; use pellets, but sparingly; a pellet every 4–6 in./10–12.5 cm. is enough.

Replacements and additions

It's inevitable that there will be casualties after planting. Occasionally a plant may just fade away instead of taking root; slugs, cats, deer, and squirrels can cause losses. Some annuals, like nemesias, are naturally relatively short-lived. In many cases, neighboring plants will quickly move in and dominate the vacant spaces, though a little encouragement may sometimes be helpful. But it can also be useful to have a few plants in reserve for any emergency gap filling.

Any spares left after planting can be moved into larger pots and kept in a sheltered place outside, and it's also worth making later sowings of particularly quick-growing plants like nemesias, mimulus and linarias – some varieties of the last two will flower in as little as six weeks from sowing and so can be very useful.

Managing growth

The intimate, intermingling planting schemes featured in this book sometimes require intervention to keep plants from overwhelming each other or to keep their growth in proportion. Snipping off shoots which are upsetting the harmony of the planting rarely leaves an ugly space for long and often the removal of a relatively substantial branch is unnoticed the next day.

But it's important to look out for this over-vigorous growth. Nasturtiums, with their dense foliage, cabbages, kales, and ornamental chards can be smothersome. The removal of a single leaf is sometimes sufficient to give neighboring plants the light they need.

Glossary

Annual A plant which completes its entire life cycle in one growing season; e.g. alyssum. Also, a seed-raised, naturally perennial plant whose useful life cycle extends only to one growing season; e.g. petunia. See also: ephemeral, winter annual.

Bedding plant Any plant set out specifically for a seasonal display then removed; e.g. impatiens, geranium.

Bicolor(ed) A flower in which two colors appear.

Biennial A plant which completes its entire life cycle over two growing seasons; e.g., foxglove. Seed germinates and the plant establishes during the summer and autumn of its first season, then flowers, sets seed and dies in its second season. Also, naturally perennial plants treated in this way: e.g., wallflower.

Calyx The group of small, leaf-like structures enclosing and protecting a flower bud; each segment is known as a sepal.

Cold frame Low structure usually with solid sides in wood, brick, concrete steel, aluminum, or sometimes plastic with a removable clear top in glass or transparent plastic. Provides protection from severe weather and used especially for hardening off (see below).

Damping off A fungus disease which attacks young seedlings, causing them to collapse and die suddenly (see page 181).

Dibber Slender device for making a planting hole in potting mix or garden soil for large seeds or for seedlings. Usually wood or plastic.

Drill Shallow furrow in garden soil made with a cane or the corner of the rake and into which seeds are sown.

Ephemeral An annual plant with a very short life cycle, often weeks. Usually a weed.

Eye The center of a flower, in a color that often contrasts with the rest of the flower.

F_1 hybrid (In this context) the result of crossing, often by hand, two specially selected and highly bred parents. The resultant plants are uniform, often very prolific. Most familiar bedding plants such as petunias, impatiens and geraniums are F_1 hybrids. Seed taken from F_1 hybrids usually produces plants unlike both the F_1 hybrid and its parents.

F_2 hybrid (In this context) the result of allowing F_1 hybrids to pollinate themselves and each other, often indiscriminately. The result is usually variable, but predictable within broad limits. The resultant plants usually retain some, but not all, of the qualities of their F_1 hybrid parents but are less expensive. Relatively few bedding plants are produced in this way but include geraniums and pansies. Plants grown from seed saved from F_2 hybrids can be variable and unpredictable.

Field grown mixture Seed collected from plants in mixed colors growing together. The resultant balance of colors is usually slightly variable and unpredictable.

Formula mixture Seed collected from plants grown separately in individual colors and blended later in a predetermined proportion. The resultant balance of colors is constant and predictable.

Fully double A flower in which the number of petals is dramatically increased so that it appears to consist entirely of petals.

Germination The development of a seed from an apparently inert object to a young plant (seedling).

Half-hardy Used to describe annual or perennial plants which thrive out-of-doors in summer but whose natural life cycle is cut short by the first autumn frosts or by low winter temperatures and must be started indoors in late winter/early spring before being planted out.

Harden off To acclimatize plants raised in a greenhouse or other protected environment to cooler conditions and more light outside by steadily exposing them to less protection.

Hardy Used to describe plants not normally killed by frosts.

Leggy Used to describe plants, especially seedlings, which have become unnaturally thin and stretched owing to their being grown in low light conditions.

Open-pollinated Of varieties derived from allowing a stand of plants to be pollinated by bees or other relatively uncontrolled means. The resulting plants vary in their uniformity according to the care with which rogues (see below) are removed.

Pelleted seed Individual seeds enclosed in a clay pellet which breaks down on contact with water. Allows very small seed to be handled and sown more easily.

Perlite White, lightweight, inert material derived from volcanic rock and used to improve drainage in potting mixes.

Picotee Used to describe flowers or petals with a pale ground color and a dark band of the same or a different color around the edge, or a dark ground with a pale band around the edge.

Pinching back (out) The removal of a shoot tip, usually from a young plant, to encourage the development of side shoots.

Plug plants Young plants, usually seedlings, grown in individual cells of potting mix enabling them to be pricked out or transplanted without disturbing the roots.

Pricking out Transferring seedlings to individual pots, or given more space in a seed tray, to allow uncrowded development.

Ray floret The colorful petals of plants in the daisy family; the central eye of daisy flowers is made up of disk florets.

Rogue An off-type, of any sort, in a stand of plants grown by a seed producer for their seed; e.g., a blue-flowered individual in a stand of plants of a white-flowered variety. If the rogue is not removed (rogued) the resulting seed will usually produce a few off-types among those which are correct when grown in the garden; e.g. blue-flowered plants among the white.

Seed crop A stand of plants grown by a seed producer specifically to provide seed.

Seed stock The batch of seed of a particular variety from a given supplier. Seed stocks from different suppliers may vary according to the attention given to roguing (see above).

Self-color Used of a flower in which the color is even, uniform and of one color.

Self-seed (n) Self-sow (v) Used when a plant in the garden sheds its own seed which then germinates nearby.

Self-fertile Used of a species or variety which will set seed when pollinated with its own pollen.

Self-sterile Used of a species or variety which will not set seed when pollinated with its own pollen.

Sepal Segment of the leaf-like structure enclosing a flower bud, collectively called the calyx.

Series A range of varieties, usually of a popular bedding plant, which are very similar in all respects except the color of their flowers.

Set seed To produce viable seed following pollination.

Space sow To place (usually large) seeds individually in the soil at consistent spacing.

Spur The slender tube at the back of some flowers, e.g., columbine, usually producing nectar.

Sterile Used of a variety or an individual plant which is incapable of producing seed. Sometimes refined as follows: male sterile, producing no viable pollen but capable of producing seed; female sterile, incapable of producing seed but producing fertile pollen.

Tender Highly susceptible to frost damage.

Thin/thin out To remove some seedlings from a row in order to allow those remaining enough space to develop without crowding.

True/true to type Of a plant, or group of plants, which matches the accepted description of the variety to which it is assumed to belong.

Variety A distinct special form of a plant which is found growing in the wild; more loosely, a distinct special form of a plant which has been selected in cultivation (more accurately known as a cultivar).

Winter annual An annual which germinates late in the growing season and flowers early the following growingseason; will also develop normally from a spring sowing.

The Problem of Names

Gardeners are often irritated or confused by botanists changing plant names, however good the reason, and in recent years changes have taken place in the botanical names for some annuals, as has been the case with other groups of plants. The situation with annuals is confused by the fact that the seed trade is even more reluctant to take up new names than other branches of the horticultural industry. The result is that new names become widely accepted in botanical literature and serious garden writing but the catalogs and seed packets stick to the old names. What's more, in different countries, different conventions are followed.

The names used in this book are not, always, absolutely botanically correct. As you will see from some of the examples on the following list, if they had been used they would have been more confusing than helpful. But it's right to give these names here so that as they become more accepted over the years gardeners will be better able to understand to which plants they refer.

So this list covers both names which are now becoming accepted and also recent changes which may take some time to become familiar. It covers both plants in this book and other annuals you may find listed in seed catalogs.

Incorrect old name	Correct new name
Althaea rosea	Alcea rosea
Alyssum maritimum	Lobularia maritima
Aster chinensis	Callistephus chinensis
Brachycome	Brachyscome
Calliopsis bicolor	Coreopsis tinctoria
Centaurea moschata	Amberboa moschata
Cheiranthus cheiri	Erysimum cheiri
Chrysanthemum carinatum	Ismelia carinata
Chrysanthemum coronarium	Xanthophthalmum coronarium
Chrysanthemum multicaule	Coleostephus myconis
Chrysanthemum nivellei	Nivellea nivellei.
Chrysanthemum paludosum	Mauranthemum paludosum
Chrysanthemum segetum	Xanthophthalmum segetum
Cineraria maritima	Senecio cineraria
Clarkia elegans	Clarkia unguiculata
Consolida ajacis	Consolida ambigua
Convolvulus major	Ipomoea purpurea
Convolvulus minor	Convolvulus tricolor
Cosmidium	Thelesperma
Delphinium zalil	Delphinium semibarbatum
Geranium peltatum	Pelargonium peltatum
Geranium × hortorum	Pelargonium × hortorum
Godetia amoena	Clarkia amoena
Godetia bottae	Clarkia bottae
Godetia grandiflora	Clarkia rubicunda
Godetia rubicunda	Clarkia rubicunda
Helichrysum bracteatum	Bracteantha bracteata
Matricaria capensis	Tanacetum parthenium
Pyrethrum ptarmiciflorum	Tanacetum prtarmiciflorum
Quamoclit coccinea	Ipomoea coccinea
Tropaeolum canariense	Tropaeolum peregrinum

Correct new name	Incorrect old name
Alcea rosea	Althaea rosea
Amberboa moschata	Centaurea moschata
Brachyscome	Brachycome
Bracteantha bracteata	Helichrysum bracteatum
Callistephus chinensis	Aster chinensis
Clarkia amoena	Godetia amoena
Clarkia bottae	Godetia bottae
Clarkia rubicunda	Godetia grandiflora, G. rubicunda
Clarkia unguiculata	Clarkia elegans
Coleostephus myconis	Chrysanthemum multicaule
Consolida ambigua	Consolida ajacis
Convolvulus tricolor	Convolvulus minor
Coreopsis tinctoria	Calliopsis bicolor
Delphinium semibarbatum	Delphinium zalil
Erysimum cheiri	Cheiranthus cheiri
Ipomoea coccinea	Quamoclit coccinea
Ipomoea purpurea	Convolvulus major
Ismelia carinata	Chrysanthemum carinatum
Lobularia maritima	Alyssum maritimum
Mauranthemum paludosum	Chrysanthemum paludosum
Nivellea nivellei	Chrysanthemum nivellei
Pelargonium peltatum	Geranium peltatum
Pelargonium × hortorum	Geranium × hortorum
Senecio cineraria	Cineraria maritima
Tanacetum parthenium	Matricaria capensis
Tanacetum prtarmiciflorum	Pyrethrum ptarmiciflorum
Thelesperma	Cosmidium
Tropaeolum peregrinum	Tropaeolum canariense
Xanthophthalmum coronarium	Chrysanthemum coronarium
Xanthophthalmum segetum	Chrysanthemum segetum

Seed Suppliers

Almost all of the seed companies supply seed by mail order; you'll also find some of these seeds on sale in garden centers. All list a good range of varieties (except where specified). Changes of address, together with details of any export arrangement, will be found at the Discovering Annuals website (see page 186).

Avant Gardens
710 High Hill Road
Dartmouth, MA 02747

Bountiful Gardens
18001 Shafer Ranch Road
Willits, CA 95490

W. Atlee Burpee & Co.
Warminster
PA 18974
http://www.burpee.com

Ferry-Morse
P.O. Box 488
Fulton
KY 42041-0488
http://gardennet.com/FerryMorse

The Flowery Branch
P.O. Box 1330
Flowery Branch
GA 30542
http://flowerybranch.com

DeGiorgio Seed Company
6011 N Street
Omaha
NE 68117-1634

Harris Seeds
60 Saginaw Drive
P.O. Box 22960
Rochester
NY 14692-2960

Johnny's Selected Seeds
1 Foss Hill Road
RR 1 Box 2580
Albion
ME 04910-9731
http://www.johnnyseeds.com

J. W. Jung Seed Co.
335 S. High Street
Randolph
WI 53957

Park Seeds Co.
1 Parkton Avenue
Greenwood, SC 29647
http://parkseed.com

Seeds of Change
P.O. Box 15700
Santa Fe
NM 87506-5700
http://www.seedsofchange.com

Seymours Selected Seeds
P.O. Box 1346
Sussex
VA 23884-0346

Shepherd's Garden Seeds
30 Irene Street
Torington, CT 06790
http://www.shepherdseeds.com

Stokes Seeds
P.O. Box 548
Buffalo
NY 14240-0548
http://stokeseeds.com

Territorial Seed Company
P.O. Box 157
Cottage Grove
OR 97424-0061
http://territorial-seed.com

Thompson & Morgan Seeds
P.O. Box 1308
22 Farraday Avenue
Jackson NJ 08527
http://www.thompson-morgan.com

World Seed
300 Morning Drive
Bakersfield
CA 93306
(for Unwins Seeds)
http://worldseed.com

Canadian mail order seed companies

The Butchart Gardens Ltd.
Box 4010
Victoria
BC V8X 2X4
http://butchartgardens.bc.ca/butchart

Florabunda Seeds
641 Rainbow Road
Salt Spring Island
BC V8K 2M7

Garden Import Inc.
P.O. Box 760
Thornhill
ON L3T 4A5
(for Suttons Seeds)
http://gardenimport.com

Seeds of Distinction
P.O. Box 86
Station A Etobicoke
Toronto
ON M9C 4V2
http://www.seedsofdistinction.com

Dig This
P.O. Box 5668
Station n B
Victoria
BC V8R 5S4

(for Sutton's Seeds: no mail order but shops in Victoria, Vancouver, Montreal, Sidney and Nanaimo – and Seattle)

British and European seed companies

Barnhaven Primroses
Langerhouad 2240
Plouzelambre France
Primroses and polyanthus only.

B&T World Seeds
Paguignan
34210 Olonzac
France
http://www.b-and-t.world.seeds.com

D.T. Brown
Station Road
Poulton-le-Fylde FY6 7HX
http://www.users.globalnet.co.uk/~dtbrown

Chiltern Seeds
Bortree Stile
Ulverston
Cumbria LA12 7PB

Mr Fothergill's Seeds
Kentford
Newmarket
Suffolk CB8 7QB

E.W. King & Co. Ltd
Monks Farm
Coggeshall Road
Kelvedon
Essex CO5 9PG

Moles Seeds
Turkey Cock Lane
Stanway
Colchester
Essex CO3 5PB
(large orders only)

Seeds-by-Size
45 Crouchfield
Boxmoor
Hemel Hempstead
Hertfordshire HP1 1PA
http://www.seeds-by-size.co.uk

Suffolk Herbs
Monks Ram
Coggeshall Road
Kelvedon, Essex CO5 9PG

Finding out more . . .

Further Reading

Books on annuals and bedding plants have been relatively few and far between and it's interesting to note that the last burst of publishing on this subject, similar to that now seen in the late 1990s, was in the mid 1950s.

In print at the time of writing

Bennet, Jennifer. *The Annual Garden* (Firefly Books, 1998)

Clark, Ethne. *Three Seasons of Summer* (Stirling Publications, 1999)

DeWolf, Gordon P. *Taylor's Guide to Annuals* (Houghton Mifflin, 1986)

Flores, Barbara. *The Great Sunflower Book* (Ten Speed Press, 1997)

Hanks, Margaret. *A Grower's Guide to Annuals* (Crescent Books, 1997)

Lloyd, Christopher and Graham Rice. *Garden Flowers from Seed* (Timber Press, 1997)

Marston, Ted. *Annuals* (Random House, 1994)

Missouri Botanic Garden Staff. *Annual Gardening* (Pantheon, 1995)

Platt, Karen, ed. *The Seed Search* (Karen Platt, (UK) 1997 and annually)

Reader's Digest, ed. *The A–Z of Annuals, Biennials and Bulbs* (Reader's Digest, 1994)

Time-Life Books, ed. *Annuals and Biennials* (Time-Life Incorporated, 1996)

Winterrowd, Wayne. *Annuals for Connoisseurs* (Prentice Hall, 1992)

All these books, together with other relevant titles published after this book went to print, are discussed on the *Discovering Annuals* website.

The Discovering Annuals website

In a unique relationship between print publishing and the World Wide Web, this book is partnered by its own dedicated website. The *Discovering Annuals* website is at

http://discoveringannuals.com

It features additional information on the plants mentioned and described in this book, together with background information for which there was unfortunately insufficient space in the book.

In addition to selected illustrated extracts from this book, The *Discovering Annuals* website also contains:

• Photographs of additional plant associations
• Additional pictures of varieties not illustrated in this book or newly introduced
• Reviews of each year's seed catalogs
• News of newly introduced varieties
• Background information on how new annuals are developed
• Reports of any new pests or diseases affecting annuals or developments in their control
• Advice on ordering seeds from British and European seed companies

The website also allows me to update information which appears in this book such as:

• Changes to seed company addresses
• Reviews of new books on annuals
• Opening times and visitor information for the recommended gardens and trial grounds
• Changes to generic and varietal names
• Changes in the availability of varieties

This is the first gardening book to be linked to a website in this way. I hope you find it useful. Please email me from the site if there are any features you would especially like to see added.

Where to see annuals

Brooklyn Botanic Garden
1000 Washington Avenue
Brooklyn, NY 11225

The Butchart Gardens, Ltd.
Box 4010, Postal Station A
Victoria, BC Canada V8X 3X4

Longwood Gardens, Inc.
Kennett Square, PA 19348

Minnesota Landscape Arboretum
University of Minnesota
3675 Arboretum Drive, Box 39
Chanhassen, MN 55317

Missouri Botanical Garden
P.O. Box 299
St. Louis, MO 63166

Montreal Botanical Garden
4101 est, rue Sherbrooke
Montreal, PQ, Canada H1X 2B2

Royal Botanical Gardens
680 Plains Road West
Burlington, ON, Canada L8N 3H8

The State Botanical Garden of Georgia
University of Georgia
2450 S. Milledge Avenue
Athens, GA 30605

Walt Disney World
P.O. Box 10000
Lake Buena Vista, FL 32830

Awards for annuals

Every year new varieties are released by plant breeders all over the world and introduced by the familiar seed companies. Many gardeners appreciate guidance as to which of these many new varieties really are worth growing.

Both in United States and in Europe there are award schemes which recognize the very best of the new introductions. Each year in the United States, All-America Selections award the very best newcomers after each year's entrants to the scheme are grown, assessed and voted upon in blind trials at sites all over the country. In Europe, Fleuroselect runs a similar scheme.

Many fine plants have received awards under these two well-established schemes. There's a full list on the *Discovering Annuals* website together with a selection of display gardens where award winners can be seen.

Index of plant names

Acknowledgments

It's customary for the author to begin this entry with the words 'This book would not have been possible without' and then list all his family, friends and relations down to the new puppy. So let's be realistic: a very different book would have been possible without anyone's help. *This* book would not have been possible without my picking the brains of all my friends in the seed trade (they're all listed on the *Discovering Annuals* website). It's not just that they've responded to my questions with as much, and occasionally more, information than commercial competitive concerns allowed. But their enjoyable enthusiasm has continually sparked mine.

I'd also like to thank photographer John Fielding, who almost every week in the summer of 1997 set his alarm clock at an utterly unreasonable hour in order to be out in my garden in the best possible light to photograph so many of the annuals for this book. John, your pictures are wonderful; thank you.

At the publishers, Frances Lincoln, I'd like to thank Erica Hunningher for her belief that the time had come for this book, Louise Kirby for her elegant design and thoughtful choice of pictures, and especially Kirsty Brackenridge for pulling it all together with such good humour and against odds which would, and indeed sometimes have, defeated lesser editors.

Finally, I want to thank jude for her constructive comments on my text, which has improved noticeably as a result, and for transforming the British edition into the American one so thoughtfully. And I'd also like to thank her for attending the 1997 Chelsea Flower Show.

Photographic Credits

(A=above, B=below, L=left, R=right)

A-Z Botanical Collection © Moira C. Smith 114
Nicola Brown 34A (Sandra and Nori Pope, Hadspen Garden)
David Cavagnaro 21, 102B
Bruce Coleman Limited/Liz Eddison 101
Eric Crichton Photos 49A, 63B, 92A, 102A, 104L, 166
John Fielding 5, 6 (Graham Rice), 7 (Graham Rice),10 (Graham Rice), 12 (Graham Rice), 18, 20 (RHS Wisley), 22-23 (N & S Pope, Hadspen Garden), 24B (Graham Rice), 25 (Graham Rice), 28-29 (Graham Rice), 30 (Graham Rice), 38A, 41 (RHS Wisley), 43 (Graham Rice), 44AR, 45, 48 (Graham Rice), 51 (Graham Rice), 52-53 (RHS Wisley), 56 (Graham Rice), 58 (RHS Wisley), 67 (Graham Rice), 71 (Graham Rice), 73B (Graham Rice), 77 (Graham Rice), 82, 89A (Graham Rice), 90 (Graham Rice), 94A, 98 (Graham Rice), 103 (Graham Rice), 107 (Graham Rice), 109 (Graham Rice), 110 (N & S Pope, Hadspen Garden), 113, 127, 135 (Graham Rice), 137 (Graham Rice), 140 (Graham Rice), 141 (Graham Rice), 142 (Graham Rice), 144-145 (Graham Rice), 151A (N & S Pope, Hadspen Garden), 153 (Graham Rice), 154 (Graham Rice), 155A (Graham Rice), 158A (Graham Rice), 159 (Graham Rice), 161 (Graham Rice), 175 Photographer/Designer John Fielding 2, 9, 13, 15, 26, 34, 37, 39, 40, 42, 50, 59, 74L, 74-75, 81, 83,85, 86, 89B, 95, 97, 111, 116, 121, 122, 123L, 147, 150, 152L, 160, 162, 163, 164A, 165, 170R, 171
John Glover 44AL, 44B, 47, 62, 64, 129A, 130-131, 132B, 133, 143, 146B, 170L
Sunniva Harte 146A, 148
Anne Hyde 124, 139
Andrew Lawson 24A, 61, 65, 66, 72, 73A, 76L, 91 (Christopher Lloyd, Great Dixter), 106R, 120B, 125A, 128, 129B, 155BL, 155BR, 156-157, 168AR, 168B, 169R
Rob Leopold 49B
Tony Lord 16-17, 19, 68-69, 173, 174
David McDonald 115
S & O Mathews 105, 167
Clive Nichols Garden Pictures 8, 63A, 84, 106L, 108B, 126, 151B
Oxford Scientific Films © Deni Bown 117, © Bob Gibbons 136
Photos Horticultural 123R
Peter Ray 32, 60
Graham Rice 1, 27, 33AL, 33B, 38B, 76R, 79, 80, 87, 92B, 93, 94B, 100, 108A, 120AL, 120AR, 125B, 132A, 138AL, 138, 152R, 158B, 164B, 168AL
Howard Rice 36, 38B, 57, 99
Derek St Romaine 31, 35, 54, 78, 88, 96, 112, 134B
Erica R. Shank 33AR, 149
Jörgen Schwartzkopf 55
Harry Smith Collection 104R
©judywhite/New Leaf Images 46, 70, 169L, 172

The publishers would like to thank the following for their help in producing this book: Anne Askwith, Jo Grey, Sarah Mitchell, Sara Robin and Ann Barratt for the index.

Editor: Kirsty Brackenridge
Art Editor: Louise Kirby
Picture Research: Sue Gladstone
Picture Editor: Anne Fraser
Editorial Director: Erica Hunningher
Art Director: Caroline Hillier